MW00876388

Steve McQueen
The Actor and His Craft

By Will Jorden

Introduction

"I live for myself and answer to nobody." -Steve McQueen

Steve McQueen was a runaway angel born in hell, one of God's creations who left his mark on audiences around the globe. A mark made with the tight smile of a dirty kid who's stolen candy and made out like a bandit.

The two most brilliant blue eyes belonged to Steve McQueen but his intensity is what made them piercing. Steve's learned ability to capture the audience's attention on camera is legendary but not until his later films did he relax into being a truly great actor. Throughout the course of his career he continued to grow as an artist, actor, and craftsman; employing the techniques introduced to him as a young man in New York City during the 1950's.

When Steve was on camera he was believable in whatever he was doing, more than that he brought authenticity to acting in a way that hadn't been before or seen since. Steve McQueen studied acting with Sanford Meisner, Uta Haggen, and Lee Strasberg, three of the most renowned acting teachers to ever live. Steve's performances are timeless lessons in the acting craft to which this book is devoted to.

Steve McQueen was never handed anything in life and that doubly applies to his acting talent. Continuing to grow and nurture his craft and learn how to best showcase himself is something he worked on his entire career. This book covers the skills and talents he used to go from being a wanderlust boy and struggling no-name actor to the highest grossing movie star in the world.

Steve remains today a quintessential idol in cinema and even holds the #10 spot in Forbes list of the Top-Earning Dead Celebrities alongside Michael Jackson, Elves Presley, Bob Marley, Marilyn Monroe, John Lennon, Albert Einstein, and Bruce Lee.

A Young McQueen.
1930-1951

"When a kid didn't have any love when he was small, he begins to wonder if he's good enough." -Steve McQueen

Six months after the start of the Great Depression, Terrence Steven McQueen was born in Beach Grove, Indiana to two alcoholic parents. Steve's father thought he'd play a good joke naming his son after a local one-armed bookie before bailing out on the family never to know his son.

As soon as he was off the bottle Steve was passed around to different caretakers when convenient so his mother, Jullian, could go back to her old life of booze and men. Many of his early childhood years were spent in Slater, Missouri with his Great Uncle Claude on a hog farm. Uncle Claude was a hard but fair man and under his care, a six-year-old Steve lived a structured life.

He would get up every day, before the sun, to do his chores then walk the two miles to and from school alone. Steve did this only to do a few more chores, his homework, eat, go to bed and do it all again the next day. He remembered this time fondly because every weekend he was able to break the routine and was given money to go see the local Saturday matinee. "Westerns were my favorite, I used to bring my cap pistol and fire at the villains," Steve recalled years later.

When Steve was eight or nine he was taken to live with Jullian and her new husband in Indianapolis but was sent back to Uncle Claude when the marriage failed soon afterward. Then when Steve was twelve he was again sent to live with Jullian and her recent husband Berri in Los Angeles. Steve was taken away from Uncle Claude and out of his stable environment once again just to be thrown into the hands of an abusive stepfather. "He apparently beat me for the sheer sadistic pleasure it gave

5

him, which included the joy he obviously derived from my pain," Steve said. "I was young. I even thought of bearing the beatings, vowing simply to hold on until I was old enough to run away. But I just couldn't. It wasn't in me. I just started fighting back."

Steve spent as little time as possible in the Berri household and found the support and acceptance he needed in a local LA street gang and his rebellious youth began. His first wife detailed in her memoirs, "To him, Los Angeles was at once fascinating, confusing, and turbulent. For the first time in his life, he found himself with an ambition. He desired to be the 'leader of the pack.' To do so, he determined he had to win the other kids' respect by becoming the 'baddest ass' of them all. If the gang leader decreed that ten hubcaps were to be stolen today by each gang member, Steve would bring back twenty. If the order of the day was for each to steal two bottles of wine, then he would just work harder and return with four. Fear of being caught just simply had to be conquered or one would miss out on what life was all about."

Witnessing her son getting into trouble with the law and beaten by her husband at home, Jullian sent Steve back to his uncle. But Steve didn't stay long and at fourteen he ran away with a traveling carnival, eventually making his way back to his mother and his gang.

All actors come to acting by different means. Marlon Brando began acting in life when, as a child, his mother would come home in a drunken stupor. Little Marlon would try and keep her coherent by impersonating neighbors or farm animals. James Dean began studying drama in High School possibly as an emotional outlet after his mother's tragic death. Steve McQueen, on the other hand, learned his acting on the streets of Los Angeles.

In Steve's last interview to a school newspaper he offered up some advice, "You should see some of life so that you can peel life, and put it to use in your acting.

Learning stuff on the streets helped my acting a lot." Pat Johnson who would become one of Steve's best friends said one reason they got along was because of their similar childhoods. "When one grows up in the streets, one learns to put on a false front and a lot of protective walls. We both felt that everyone was potentially a con man, and you had to ensure you were never 'had'. You never fully trusted anybody, and you never showed any weakness. If you show weakness in the streets, you're dead. The less a person knew about you, the safer you were. On the streets is where you perfected your con. If you wanted something from somebody, you acted a certain way. You learned how to adjust, how to adapt, and playing different roles was how you survived. This I can tell you: Steve McQueen was an actor long before he ever came to Hollywood."

Eventually, his life with his gang got him in trouble one too many times and Steve wound up as #3188 at the Chino Hills Boys Republic reform school. When he got there his roommate recalled, "[Steve] was cut off emotionally and he was guarded, just like me. If I asked him a question, most likely I wasn't going to get an answer, so I didn't ask. Steve was the one who did the approaching if he wanted something. Reflecting back, he was emotionally in pain, and when I later saw him on screen, his independence and pain were real. There was always anger under the surface, and you can see the tragedy of his life in his films, which made him so compelling."

Before he could make his way onto the big screen he'd first have to get through the Boys Republic who's motto is, "Nothing Without Labor." In-between classes and farm work Steve attempted two breakouts as if he was preparing for his role in *The Great Escape*.

But after being in their system for a few months Steve finally received some good news, Jullian was coming to bring him home for the holidays. He packed his bag and got up early in the morning to wait for her on the front porch. Steve sat there and watched as the other families came for their boys but Steve's mother was a no show. He sat there till ten at night, marking one of his lowest points of his life. That's when guidance counselor Lloyd Panter took the task upon him self to bring Steve out of this hole.

"Understanding is the magic word. That's something more important than love. And it ought to be easier to give," Steve said. "You don't have to beat your heart out to give someone understanding. Mr. Panter helped change my life. He didn't give me love, but he did give me understanding. It was enough."

Steve started turning his life around after that, he stopped trying to run away and became an active member in the Boys Republic community and was even elected to the prestigious Boys Council. Panter was telling Steve, "Give life an honest shot. You could be somebody special someday." And Steve was listening, "No one seemed to give a damn about my future life as an adult—but he did, and it meant a lot to me."

Panter even gave Steve an introduction to the works of William Shakespeare. Although the capacity to which he did is unclear, Steve later noted, "In that way, he laid the foundation for my later interest in theater."

After 14 months at the Boys Republic, Steve was released. Jullian sent him a Grey Hound bus ticket and five dollars so he could transverse the country to live with her and her new fiancé in New York City. Steve made the journey at 16 years old with almost nothing but the clothes on his back and the pocket watch his uncle Claude had given him many years before.

But any thoughts of his mother changing her old ways were shattered when he stepped off the bus. He could smell alcohol on her breath and found out he wouldn't be living with her after all. Jullian had found Steve an apartment where he would be living with two gay men; although she failed to mention that part and Steve was in for a surprise when he returned home one night.

Seeing old patterns resurface Steve left town on a whim finding work on a tanker leaving for the Dominican Republic. When he got there he then found work as a towel boy in a brothel, which apparently he enjoyed very much always recounting the tales with a twinkle in his eye. After two months he continued his travels making his way to the Texas oil fields as a laborer, worked as a lumberjack in Canada, and hustled pens down the east coast to Myrtle Beach South Carolina.

At 17 years old Steve was tired of running. He had experienced more out of life than most people twice his age and was now looking for a stable environment to call home. That's when he decided to join the Marines. With a name tag that read, "T.S. McQueen" Steve acquired the nickname, "Tough Shit," which is impressive seeing how most of those Marines at that time were battle hardened WWII veterans of the Pacific Theater.

Steve had as many adventures in the Marines as was congruent with the rest of his life leading up to that point. But for Steve, his time in the Marines turned out to be similar his time spent in The Boys Republic. When he first went in he caused a lot of trouble and got into a lot of trouble. He even went AWOL a few times to visit girlfriends but once he was able to adjust to the system he turned things around for himself. Steve said of his service, "The Marines gave me discipline I could live with. By the time I got out, I was able to cope with things on a more realistic level. All in all, despite my problems, I liked being in the Marines."

Steve was honorably discharged in April of 1950 and looking for his next adventure he thought he'd give New York City another try. At the time NYC was the hub of the beatnik renaissance and Greenwich Village was the epicenter. The Village in the 50's was a very special time and place to be a part of in American history as well as in Steve's life, "For the first time in my life I was really exposed to music, culture, a little kindness, a little sensitivity."

Greenwich Village wasn't a place people pilgrimaged to simply because there wasn't any media hype. Instead, this is where the cool people–those moody street irregulars and the loose creative types bedded themselves. The Village became a little corner of the world for true individuals looking to express themselves and have a little fun. McQueen fit right in, "It was a time when people lived there because they were broke, not because it was fashionable. You could live in a cold water flat for twenty-three bucks a month, no questions asked, and the bathroom was in the hall."

Shirtless and wearing Levi's jeans Steve would leave his 5th-floor walk-up cold-water flat at night and fire up his Indian motorcycle. He'd aim the beast down the narrow city streets, revving up the engine and booming past taverns, theaters, and coffeehouses. Maybe he didn't always know where he was going but he was sure to find the people as wild as he was. "Things happened in the Village," Steve said. "Good things. Bad things. People expected you to be a little off-center when you lived there. The chicks were wilder and the pace was faster. I dug it."

Steve had finally found an environment that could match his own high-octane energy and intensity but he had no direction. He had a lot of jobs during this time but with only a 9th-grade education level the jobs he got reflected that and didn't challenge him in any way other than his patience. And without the stern direction of the Boys Republic or the Marines, Steve began stealing again. "I asked myself the bitter question, 'Man, where are you going? When are you gonna get with it?' and I had no answer. Talk about beat! I was it!"

Steve's Early Acting Training.
1951-1955

"I took stock of myself. I'd drifted around so much that I knew I'd have to start on the ground floor of any career I took up, so why not with acting? Anyway, one day I telephoned Meisner." -Steve McQueen

Steve was thinking of learning tile setting as his next throw away job when suddenly everyone in his life started pushing him to go into acting. And into the hands of the legendary teacher Sanford Meisner no less. Good friend Mark Rydell and Steve's girl at the time, Donna Barton, helped guide him there but Victor Lukens was probably the one most influential on getting Steve to pursue a career in acting. Victor was a director of cinematography and Jullian's boyfriend at the time. He took a liking to Steve and started bringing Steve to film sets, even getting him in front of the camera a few times. Once Steve showed a real interest and knack for acting Victor thought the best thing to do was to get him in touch with his good friend Sanford Meisner.

Theatre's best-kept secret was acting teacher and guru Sanford Meisner, the Yoda of the acting world. In 1931 Sandy was one of the actors who joined the legendary Group Theater in the companies first year where he and the other core members revolutionized American theater acting. When the Group Theater disbanded Sandy became head of the acting program at the Neighborhood Playhouse in New York City.

"I remember walking towards his office, telling myself it was a hundred to one against me having the talent to break through," Steve recalled. "But I also figured that here was my chance, and I had plenty of energy and ambition. A secretary showed me into Meisner's office. He shook hands and said, 'Mr. McQueen pleased to meet you."

11

Sandy remembered meeting Steve that day saying, "He was an original - both tough and childlike, like Marilyn Monroe, as if he'd been through everything but had preserved a certain basic innocence. I accepted him at once."

Steve was one of the lucky ones as only 71 of 3,000 applicants were accepted that year. He found himself in an exclusive club training alongside some of the most talented and dedicated actors New York had to offer. Steve had never done any real acting before so Sandy's choice to accept him into his class could seem out of place but Sandy's assistant Wynn Handman said, "Meisner preferred what he called 'untutored' students so that he could train them from the start to avoid bad habits. Steve didn't have any that I recall, but it did take some effort to reach him on a personal level."

If Steve was looking for the next challenge in his life and he found just that at The Neighborhood Playhouse. Paul Morrison who was the school administrator went before the students on the first day after the student's introductions and told them plainly, "This is a school with no fancy frills. You'll all work hard; lateness is inexcusable. At the end of the first year, about half of you will not return. Those of you who make it through the second year and finish the course will be well trained."

"Take it from a Director: If you get an actor that Sandy Meisner has trained, you've been blessed." -Elia Kazan

On his first day of class, Mr. Meisner would lead off with a simple exercise asking all the students to close their eyes and listen to the sounds of the NYC traffic in an attempt to memorize everything they heard. Mr. Meisner was teaching them that "The foundation of acting is the reality of doing." When the exercise was over the students realized they didn't need to create a character in order to listen and they also didn't need to be intellectual about the activity or pretend to listen as many actors do. The students simply needed to do the activity and let go of everything else. This would lead into Sanford Meisner's definition of acting, "Acting is the ability to live truthfully under the given imaginary circumstances."

In order to foster living truthfully on the stage, Meisner's students learn behavioral repetition exercises designed so that the actor can put all their attention onto the other person, just like when all of their attention was on listening to the sounds of traffic. This allows them to live in the moment and freely act on their impulses. Sandy designed his "Word Repetition Game" saying, "I decided I wanted an exercise for actors where there is no intellectuality. I wanted to eliminate all that 'head' work, to take away all the mental manipulation and get to where the impulses come from."

Steve proved to be a natural and grabbed the attention of future Academy Award winner Eli Wallach who was training alongside Steve, "Even then McQueen had the raw skill. His chief talent lay in being observant. What McQueen had learned to do was what separates the true artist from mediocrity: to watch and, above all, to listen."

Steve's ability to watch and listen was cultivated during his youth. Spending so much time on the streets in the gutter of life meant he was constantly around con men so reading people was a necessity of his survival. With Sandy's Word Repetition Game, Steve was able to transfer these skills over to acting.

The Independent Activities that the students learn next, get them as actors to commit 100% to an activity that's difficult if not almost impossible to do. The students pick activities that range from memorizing a Presidential speech in a short amount of time to gluing a shattered vase back together perfectly.

Once the students can do the Word Repetition Game and Independent Activities separately the two exercises are then combined into one. The two actors on stage must listen and answer each other while one of them performs a difficult activity, (which under normal circumstances would take all their attention). Steve and the other students learn to take in and juggle all of these elements at once for the sole purpose of being able to live truthfully under the given imaginary circumstances.

Over the course of two years, more and more elements are added to these improvisations that make them complete scenes with objectives, emotional elements from the imagination, relationships, and impediments.

"If you'll stay with it, McQueen, you can make it." -Sanford Meisner

Gregory Peck who took Sandy's class in the 1930's said, "I don't think I was ever comfortable. No, I think it was two years of stress and strain almost unrelieved. Some moments were better than others. Once in a while, you'd do an improvisation and get a slight nod of approval from Sandy and that would be a red letter day. And there were other days when it was a disaster."

One of Steve's disaster days happened when he and a female partner were doing an improvisation on the stage. The two were entrenched in an argument when she had the impulse to slap Steve, which she acted upon. "I couldn't stand it, Steve said. "I hit back as hard as I could and knocked her cold. Man, it was Panicksville!" When she came to Steve was the one who was the most shaken and he stopped coming to class because of what he had done. But Sandy was supportive and was able to talk him into coming back.

Any psychologist who's looked at Steve's past will say that throughout his life Steve was constantly looking for a father figure. He found one in Sandy and although Sandy could be hard he was a fair man and Steve respected him. "Until [Meisner] got after me I understood nothing," McQueen said. "Raw talent must be channeled carefully or it can be ruined. Meisner knew just how to bring out the best in me, and he made me look deep into myself and face up to my potentials as well as my limitations. And let me tell you, I was no prize package for any teacher. I used to sit at the back of the class and talk to nobody. Meisner gradually wend me out of that shell."

Many of Steve's classmates were surprised when he became so successful later in life. They recognized that when he put in the effort he was compelling but every once in a while they found him asleep in class or absent altogether. What they didn't know was that outside of class Steve had a full-time job as a truck driver. While the other students went home in the evening and went to bed Steve was making nightly deliveries and often was only able to get a single hour of sleep before class the next day.

More often than not, however, Steve brought the same level of intensity to class as he did from past areas of his life. Like when he was a troubled youth stealing twice as many hubcaps as the other boys; here Steve was bringing to class twice as many improvisations as his fellow classmates because in his mind he simply had to be the best.

Most of the public regards actors as a sort of romantic figure whereas Steve, even as a successful actor himself, referred to most actors as having "Candy-ass acting." But as Steve participated in class he began to learn that acting is very much a craft to be worked on and developed.

Nightly at the Neighborhood Playhouse, the students challenge themselves and each other to reveal those hard-hitting deep emotions that people seldom experience. Emotional work involving the loss of a loved one or a dramatic break up could have an actor sobbing uncontrollably or slamming the stage door shut out of genuine rage. Yet another scene could have an actor jumping around the stage, singing, and laughing hysterically having imagined they just won the lottery. There's a lot of self-discovery during these exercises, some positive and some negative but all of which is used artistically.

A tremendous amount of courage is required to reveal oneself so candidly to the possible criticism and judgment of others. Something had to be driving Steve for him to complete the program. Students that can't handle the experience start to put in less effort over time before they leave altogether or are not asked to return for the second year. Steve was not only asked to return by Sandy but a talent agent tempted him with fame and fortune as long as he focused on auditions instead of class. Steve turned the agent down saying, "Not yet. I'm still a student." Steve knew that being at the Neighborhood Playhouse was exactly where he needed to be.

The full two years of training Steve put into graduating at the Neighborhood Playhouse became the first thing in his life that Steve didn't run away from. "I know that when I was studying in New York, I knew that I couldn't afford to fail because it was the only thing that I knew how to do and that I didn't know any other trade, but then I really, I do enjoy acting. I think it's a great craft, you know? I mean, it's a marvelous kind of feeling." Steve fell in love with acting but there were more challenges ahead.

"He was badly educated, defensive, hostile." -Uta Hagen

After Steve graduated, Sanford Meisner recommended he study under the equally legendary Uta Hagen. Steve was ready for his next challenge but as a student under Uta, Steve lost his direction. Edward Morehouse who now teaches at the school witnessed Steve at this time, "When it came to class, he wasn't that serious. He was lazy and poorly disciplined, but he didn't sit around boasting about how fabulous he was either, as many actors do." One thing or another was pulling Steve out of taking his training under Uta seriously.

Like Sandy, Uta was also a revered and demanding acting teacher. Both could get riled up and yell out of passion but the two have completely different personalities and teaching styles. Sandy was very gentle and made his students feel like he was on their side, he would critique an actor's work but never the actor himself. Uta, on the other hand, could devastate a student with her personal criticisms. Steve was full of dogged sensitivities that followed him from his youth and he may have been too disheartened by her criticisms to fully commit to her and her teachings.

A clash of personalities between Steve and Uta may have also caused a rift. Steve didn't take too kindly to authority figures; he was a natural nonconformist whereas Uta loved structure and discipline. Steve didn't help the situation either by disrespecting his classmates. He slept with many of the female students and began bragging about the sexcapades in class.

If that wasn't enough the technique itself is a much more intellectual approach to acting whereas Sandy at the Neighborhood Playhouse tried to remove intellectually from his students. Morehouse noted on Steve's participation, "All the things we were taught to do, he didn't seem to want to do. We were told to work on this or that, and we did, and Steve didn't." For whichever reason Steve didn't apply himself in Uta's class and soon he was on the lookout for a new place to continue his acting training.

"At the beginning, back in '51, I had to force myself to stick with [acting]. I was real uncomfortable, real uncomfortable." -Steve McQueen

In the 1950s' there was no greater test of acting merit than becoming a member of the Actor's Studio, a challenge Steve couldn't pass up. Only the best actors get in and join the ranks of Marlon Brando, Montgomery Clift, and the new talk of the town—James Dean. Steve picked a scene from *Golden Boy* to perform for his entry audition and out of the 2,000 actors who auditioned that year only Steve McQueen and another young man, Martin Landau, were accepted.

The Actor's Studio was run by Lee Strasberg who was one of three founding members of the Group Theater and is now considered the "father of method acting in America."

Steve was a little more disciplined in Lee's class than he was in Uta's but he didn't fully commit to the program, nor was he required to. The Actors Studio is different than the other acting schools because the students there are considered more as members and can come and go, work or not work as they please, which Steve took advantage of. Steve chose to attend classes but never act in any scenes because of how intimidating he found Lee's critiquing.

How intimidating could he be? James Dean found that out the hard way when he was devastated by Lee after a scene, from that point on James never performed a scene there again. Steve jokingly said in regards to scene work done in front of Lee, "I would rather take my chances with the paying public."

In Lee Strasberg's Method, actors are encouraged to create detailed backstories for their characters to help them get into the mindset of the person they're playing. They're trained in relaxation as well as concentration techniques to help facilitate the reliving of past emotions. Past emotions they can then inject into their acting, a

18

technique known as "emotional recall."

Students in Lee's class even develop their five senses so that they may vividly relive and not just remember an emotional experience they once had. The goal is to substitute what the actor believes their character should be feeling with the emotion the actor experienced in the past. This is a key difference between The Actor's Studio and what Steve learned at the Neighborhood Playhouse. Sanford Meisner teaches that an actor's emotional truth comes from his present imagination whereas Strasberg teaches that emotional truth comes from resurrecting an actor's past feelings.

Over the course of his time there Steve became disillusioned with the Actors Studio and he began having many of the same problems he had when he was in Uta's class. John Gilmore who was a student in the class remembers how things transpired in the end, "Strasberg made an announcement during class that 'certain individuals' could no longer feel welcome as members of the studio's close-knit family. Lee said, 'They prefer the empty glittering to dedicating themselves to the hard work committed here. A rattlesnake cannot be aligned with the heart of the family." And with that Steve McQueen became the only person to ever be kicked out of the Actors Studio.

Steve used some of what he learned from the Actors Studio in his war films *Hell is for Heroes* and *The War Lover* but the techniques took an emotional toll on him and he never specifically applied them again. Jackie Gleason who starred alongside Steve the next year in *Soldier in the Rain* stated, "Whatever he learned there, it doesn't show on him." And Steve himself acknowledged, "I used to be a Method School cowboy, and I think a lot of Stanislavski is so much Bull-ovslavski. So as far as I'm concerned, acting for the movies is mainly intuition."

"I'm an intuitive actor, I mean, I couldn't sit and talk about acting and say, this is what I do because I don't really know." -Steve McQueen

There's an old acting proverb that says, "One day an actor forgot his lines and thus naturalism was born." The truth is more deliberate than that and one early recording of an actor taking a more naturalistic approach is in the 1883 essay, *On The Actors Art*. The essay details the history of French actor Le Kain who brought authenticity to his acting in the '1700s' when stage acting was grandiose and anything but natural.

Le Kain's naturalistic approach was rejected and dismissed by his peers until one night he performed for King Louis XV. His performance was so powerful compared to the other actors that the King praised him, "This man has made me weep. I who never weep."

At that time an actors projection of speech was the art form and actors practiced reciting verse with varying levels of emphasis. Le Kain's revelation was that in order to move an audience emotionally the actor had to first be moved himself. He used nature as his model to be natural and attempted to recreate actions, inflections, and looks precisely as they happen in real life.

The American acting techniques Steve learned follow Le Kain's lead but are much more internal about the process. By becoming emotionally full and reacting truthfully an actor doesn't need to worry about recreating life because they'll be living in the moment.

Many fans of McQueen would go on to praise his ability to express himself through a particular look or gesture. But to think he was solely focused on his external appearance doesn't give him enough credit. Steve was trained to be an intuitive actor and work from the inside-out, "I try very hard to try and get it out of myself. I don't like acting when it's playing house, I try to extract out of my life the same reality that I'm existing in."

Steve's Fledgling Career.
1955-1958

"I've got to make it. You're going to make it! You have to make it, man!" -Steve McQueen to himself in a mirror as noted by a girlfriend.

The more Steve failed to connect with his new acting teachers the way he did with Sandy the more he started auditioning for plays. Martin Landau said, "Make no mistake Steve's goal was to be a working actor on Broadway. Steve was one of the people trying to get work, who were wonderfully gifted, and years later became iconic and legendary. But at the time we were all kind of scrambling."

Steve's training was giving him a solid basis for his acting craft but his first paid gig doing Yiddish theater didn't go so well. Steve proved to have a little more confidence than actual live theater experience and the young hopeful with only one line was fired after four performances. "I guess it was my lousy Yiddish," he joked.

But not long after and only five years after his first acting lesson Steve McQueen's name was in lights over Broadway. Steve replaced Ben Gazzara in *A Hatful of Rain* playing a Korean War veteran addicted to heroin. For the role, the playwright encouraged Steve to hang out with real junkies which he did. *Variety* called his interpretation "effective," which isn't the most gratifying word an actor wants to hear describing his performance but the magazine confessed that this role would even be difficult for an actor of more experience.

Getting on Broadway gave Steve the legitimacy he needed to move his life in another direction as well, he was going to ask a special little "chickie" out on a date. Neile Adams was a young, highly successful Broadway actor/singer/dancer and the two had been eyeing each other for weeks. Steve waited to ask her out until after his first performance of *A Hatful of Rain* so that he could officially say he was a Broadway actor like her.

In their first date, Steve surprised Neile by picking her up on his motorcycle when she was walking out of Carnegie Hall. "Put your left arm around my wrist, hold your skirt down with your right hand, and hold onto your heels," Steve commanded. "Now, where do you live? You've got to change into something more comfortable. We're going down to the Village."

They spent the night going to different coffee shops telling each other about their lives and the more they talked the more they realized they had in common. Neile began to realize something about Steve no one ever had, "I saw innocence in his eyes and heard it in his voice. You see, he really didn't know what love was. And hope was something that he dismissed as a trick by others to soften him up. He was so tough, so ready to tear the world apart at the slightest provocation, so sure that life was one long dogfight. Yet for all the ugliness that smeared his life, he was an innocent man. He had never known the meaning of love and hope. It's what I saw at that instant that made me cry. He didn't know love and hope because no one had ever loved him. No one had ever given him hope."

Neile would be the first woman to ever give Steve love and hope, and this bad boy who initially told her "I ain't the marrying kind," married her four months later. And in marrying Neile he made the greatest career move of his life. She became his most trusted confidant throughout his career and she was able to coach him and help find his onscreen persona.

Steve landed his first film role in a small part opposite Paul Newman in *Somebody Up There Likes Me*. Steve learned quickly he liked film much more than theater and film suited him because the camera could get in much closer whereas Steve tended to wash out on stage. "He

22

liked this medium better than the others," Neile said. "However, when I saw the movie, I had to tell him just how awful he was. At that point, he was not sure whether he was Marlon Brando or James Dean, so he wound up imitating both and showed absolutely nothing of himself. But he would learn. He could accept constructive criticism, especially when he knew we were on the same team."

Neile was also making plays to her representatives to take Steve on as a client. Her agents at the William Morris Agency and her press agents were quick to please their female star and agreed. Neile's talent manager Hilly Elkins, on the other hand, wasn't so enthusiastic after meeting him and told her plainly, "There are too many blond-haired, blue-eyed boys in Hollywood. I can't handle him."

Wanting to please Neile, however, Hilly did get Steve a role on *The Defender* starring Ralph Bellamy and a young William Shatner. Neile didn't waste this opportunity either, "This was the first time I had been with him through the very early stages of production and I was able to drop a gentle hint here and there about how he shouldn't play this role based on the work I'd seen him do in *Somebody Up There Likes Me* and *A Hatful of Rain*. For instance, he had a wonderful smile and a delightful childlike sense of humor. I asked him if maybe when he did his scenes with his mother he could show the audience that smile. His role of the convicted murderer was heavy, but I felt that a motivation could be found to give the character another color and another shade. He saw what I was talking about, and indeed his scenes with Vivian Nathan, who played his mother, were poignant simply because he showed no self-pity. And for the very first time, the viewing public was allowed a peek into his bad-boy personality."

In the Meisner technique, character work is done towards the end of the program because if an actor concerns himself with creating a character too early then the results are fake as seen in Steve's earlier roles. Neile picked up where Sanford Meisner left off and helped Steve present his own character on camera. And as the legendary writer and director, David Mamet says, "Character is habitual action driven from will, it is not how someone holds a handkerchief." Mamet in his book *True And False* goes on to say that character for the stage and screen is actually an illusion created by uniting the courage of the actor with the lines written by the playwright.

Another important aspect of this particular role was that the part was perfectly suited to him. Steve didn't have to overextend in any way; the role was that of a street kid in a tough situation who could lose his temper but never his code of ethics. This is a role Steve would play throughout his career. And the way he approached the role was summed up by his co-star William Shatner, "I remember watching McQueen and thinking, 'Wow, he doesn't do anything.' He was inarticulate, he mumbled, and only later did I understand how beautifully he did nothing. It was so internalized that the camera picked it up as would a pair of inquisitive eyes. Out of seemingly nothing he was creating a unique form of reality."

The Defender was well received and the *New York Daily News* wrote, "The acting was uniformly expert. Bellany, Martin Balsam and especially McQueen." He even got fan mail and for the first time Steve was being noticed for something other than his bad habits. Neile's manager Hilly Elkins happened to be watching TV the night the show aired, "I saw one minute of *The Defender* and he just broke through the screen. Those eyes just really came out at you." He imminently called up Neile and told her, "I'm very wrong about Steve and I'm sorry. I'd be glad to sign him."

Steve now had a complete team of representatives helping him find work, stay in the public eye, and negotiate deals for him. But he also had a loving woman backing him up with a brilliant eye for how to best show off her husband to the world.

Wanted: Dead or Alive season 1
1958-1959

"I needed a little guy who looked tough enough to get the job done but with a kind of boyish appeal behind the toughness. He had to be vulnerable, so the audience would root for him against the bad guys." -Producer Vincent Fennerlly

By the end of 1958, the western genre had transited from movies to television, so much so that one-third of network television featured the old west. Steve's manager Hilly Elkins thought a similar transition for Steve would benefit his career and he set out to do just that.

Hilly deserves all the credit for getting Steve his own television series. When CBS and Four Star Studios were looking for an actor to head the spin-off of *Trackdown*, their most popular TV western, they turned to Hilly Elkins. Hilly managed the star of *Trackdown* and was able to persuade the studio executives that McQueen was just the actor they were looking for.

As a test of Steve's potential, he was featured in two episodes of *Trackdown* in which he played three different characters. Steve's acting in the first episode is quite possibly his worst on-screen performance of his entire career. He's dull, rigid, and completely one-dimensional. In the second episode, however, he was absolutely wonderful. Steve played twin brothers at odds with one another. In this episode, his acting is much more relaxed and he delivers two compelling performances subtly differentiating the brothers by making one tougher and sure of himself and the other one a little more naive and vulnerable.

The producer of *Trackdown* and a new show *Wanted Dead or Alive*, Vincent Fennelly, liked the duality he saw in Steve and said, "I chose him because he was so ordinary. Bounty hunters have it bad, you know. Everyone is against them, except the viewer. Steve McQueen was no beauty but he had this kind of animal instinct; he could purr and show his claws at the same time." CBS also gave their stamp of approval on Steve and the show *Wanted: Dead or Alive* went into production.

"[Randall] seemed to be a loner, a guy who made his own decisions, and he didn't have a big star on his chest. This appealed to me." -Steve McQueen

In the series Steve plays, Josh Randall, a civil war veteran who after his side lost the war found work as a bank clerk. As the story goes, one day he looked up through the bars protecting him and realized he was in a prison of his own doing. He quit that afternoon and began collecting the bounties on wanted men he'd bring to the authorities.

As a bounty hunter, Josh Randall is hated by lawbreakers, despised by Sheriffs, and looked down upon by townspeople everywhere. And yet Randall is making the West a safer place to be, going places the town Sheriffs can't or aren't willing to go, pulling dangerous wanted men from the cracks and crevasses of the old west.

Steve portrays Randall as a man driven by a strict moral code with an unwavering capacity to not pass judgment. He always prefers to bring a wanted person in alive when bringing them in dead would be, not only lawful but safer for him.

Josh isn't bringing in these people for charity work, however, he expects to get paid and paid in full. Sometimes he donates the money to someone in need but his righteous sense of getting paid is just as big as the sawed-off rifle strapped to his hip.

Bringing this role to life was something that Steve became very passionate about and he didn't mind fighting producers, writers, and directors over his interpretation of Randall. A small example of this is the hat he chose to wear, "They thought all cowboys had shiny new saddles and their hats were never crumpled. What real cowboy has a shiny new hat, I ask you?"

"The fans don't care if there is violence in their TV western fare—what they want most is action, and the action must be sustained or there is a quick twist of the dial." -Steve McQueen

Wanted Dead or Alive first aired on September 6, 1958, and a young wide-eyed 5-year-old girl snuck out of bed and walked downstairs to watch the show that was forbidden for her. "I was mesmerized by the blond-haired, blue-eyed star of the show. Steve's portrayal of Josh Randall, a tough-as-nails bounty hunter who was a brooding loner, was tempered by his vulnerability and his underdog status. I don't know what it was about him - the special "Maire's Laig" gun he used on his tormentors, his sexy half-grin or that he was a man of few words, but I was entranced."

That little girl would grow up to be Steve's third wife but that would be many years down the line. The first critic reviews weren't as positive however and mostly focused on the violence. But those critics weren't in tune with audiences and like the little girl, audiences loved Steve and they loved the show. *Wanted Dead or Alive* quickly rose to one of the top ten most watched series on television at the time.

Neile noted, "These early reviews only made Steve more determined than ever to mold his character to his liking. He felt that Josh Randall had to display some human frailties in order to make the man more believable, more likable, and more vulnerable. He felt that John

Wayne's sort of bravura was not compatible with this sort of hero. Actually, he was paving the way for the growth of Steve McQueen as an actor."

With an almost religious fervor, Steve began a campaign to mold the series to his ideals for the rest of the first season. He started having people fired and being a stunt man or a director didn't matter to him, if Steve felt someone didn't bring the right attitude and ideals then they were off his show.

Steve's manager explained that his behavior didn't come from the ego of a self-righteous star, "Every bit of energy he expended was designed to make a better show." This is the moment in McQueen's career when he took the reins of his destiny and went down the path to his ultimate legendary status. Steve's further involvement in the show didn't make him popular with those he worked with but his instincts made the show better, improving the ratings and bringing more people to tune in Saturday nights.

Steve's ideas for how to define the show and Josh Randall didn't come from nowhere. He pulled them from his own personality and life experience. Neile explains. "The scripts being given him were too unrealistic. The 'superman' sort of Westerns were passé as far as Steve was concerned. When the script called for Josh to do battle with three giant gunmen or was told to 'grit' by a group of desperadoes, Steve's instinct told him the character should react the way Steve himself would. That is, to 'grit' and then come back and shoot them in the back if necessary."

Steve told one of his directors, "Look, I'm not going to fight a guy who's eight feet tall or shoot it out with Billy the Kid. If somebody pushes me too far so that I don't have anywhere to go, I'm going to fight with him, and I'll get him any way I can. If I rip his ear off or put his eye out, that's the ball game. I don't play around. I want to win."

Neile accounts a story that Steve loved telling when he was in the Marines where two guys were giving him a hard time, "A fistfight was about to ensue when Steve bowed out, recognizing that he wouldn't be able to handle the two capably. Instead, he waited in the latrine and when one of them came in he said, 'Hey, you!' When the lone man turned, 'I punched him and kicked the hell out of him. I made my point and was never bothered again.'"

By Steve bringing in his real world experiences into the show he brought a realism that, at the time, was radical.

"When a horse learns to buy martinis, I'll learn to like horses." -Steve McQueen

Nothing was going to stop Steve and no one's job was safe, not even his horses' job. For the first six episodes, Steve had a horse that didn't match his own intensity. "They gave me this real old horse they had put on roller skates and pushed on the sound stage," Steve said. "I went to [producer] Dick Powell and said, 'Listen, let me pick out my own horse. We're going to be doing this series for a while; I'd kind of like a horse I got something going with, you know?'

"So I went to a friend of mine, a cowboy I knew, and I asked him if he had any good quarter horses. He said, 'Yeah', and we looked at a sorrel, and a dapple gray, and they had a white palomino. They also had this black horse that the cowboy was working. I said, 'This one,' and I pointed to the black horse. I got on him and he bucked me off right away. So this decided me. I wouldn't have any other horse." That horse's name was Ringo and they would battle each other over the next 88 episodes together.

Their first week of shooting together set the tone for the three seasons to come. Ringo turned out to be a nightmare quickly kicking out four or five lights as well as kicking and biting the other horses. Steve wasn't left out either. Throughout the first season, Steve was bitten multiple times and even had his big toe broken when Ringo stamped his foot. Of course Steve was never one to back down from a fight. Steve's publicist David Foster recalled, "It was wild. This horse was getting pretty nervous under the lights and all, so the dumb beast balked and stepped on Steve's foot. So Steve balled up his fist and punched the fucker right in the snout."

"For three long years that horse and I fought like fanatics, both of us bent on winning," Steve said. "He'd step on me. On purpose, again and again. And I'd punch him each time for stepping on me, but he would do it again. We never did compromise, and I sort of liked the idea that he would never compromise. The son-of-a-bitch, no matter how much he was paid back in kind, he stood his place. And we really loved each other, but he never surrendered and this is how he taught me a lesson. He proved better than me and smarter."

Wanted Dead or Alive wasn't an easy show to make. Steve explained "You don't have any idea what a rough grind it is, doing a TV series. I had to be up at 5:00 A.M., to the studio by 6:30 A.M. Then worked all day on the set and usually didn't get home till 9:00 P.M. Sometimes, under deadline pressure, we'd film a whole episode in a single day!" And working like this went on for months.

Even when they weren't under deadline pressure filming an episode only took 3 days, which is why they made over 90 episodes in three seasons. 1950's television serials were notorious for compromising quality for quantity. Examples of this are seen throughout production. Almost every episode was shot at the Selznick Studio in Hollywood so every episode looks like Randall is riding into the same town only with different names painted on the buildings. Even worse many of the same

31

actors are cast as different characters episode to episode. James Coburn who will star alongside McQueen in *The Magnificent Seven* was cast as an eye-patch-wearing bad guy in episode #21 then recast as Randall's good old buddy in episode #30, minus the eye patch.

In order to save money the studio filmed as quickly as possible, which meant that Steve was always being rushed. "They'd roll the cameras before I was ready. Everybody was jumping on me, trying to change me as an actor. So finally I just said, 'Stuff it,' you know. I gave my gun to the assistant director and said, 'Here man, you do it.' Then I went home to my old lady and said, 'Hey, baby, let's go to Australia."

McQueen got his point across but the head of Four Star Studios wasn't afraid to put Steve in his place either. Head-honcho Dick Powell told Steve on one occasion, "We are a bakery, and you are the product. We tell you how you're wrapped, presented, and sold, and that's how the cookie crumbles."

"Any actor who works on a TV show and just takes home the money every week is crazy. I mean, this is a great opportunity to learn your craft. Emotionally, it's important for me to be a good actor. I don't want to be second best."
-Steve McQueen

As grueling as the filming was Steve was finally bringing in the big bucks, $750 an episode. More importantly, the first season provided Steve the opportunity to practice and develop his acting skills. Although Steve spent two years learning the Meisner technique and had numerous acting jobs before *Wanted*, this was the first time Steve was consistently in front of a camera.

On the set Steve learned more than simple acting, he was also learning the technique for the camera. Felice

Orlandi said, "Steve learned what very few actors know to do: he learned the camera. He knew that it took just a certain kind of subtle look to express a certain emotion where most actors tend to over exaggerate. He really knew his job when he was in front of the camera, and that's a mystery for a lot of actors."

Neile said he would experiment a lot while on camera to see what came across and thus what worked. And with a better understanding, Steve was better able to communicate his role and bring the story to life. In one episode Steve enters a fancy restaurant, not the normal haven for a seasoned bounty hunter, to which Steve is able to communicate this with nothing but his hat and subtle mannerisms.

His behavior on screen shows that he knows to remove his hat when entering the fancy restaurant but once he gets seated at his table he's left puzzled. Steve as Randall rather awkwardly looks around the table, switching his hat from one hand to the other as his eyes shift to every possible place he could put his hat. When his server arrives Randall's mouth hangs open as he looks to the man for direction but the waiter ignores him dispensing pleasantries. Randall then quickly discerns there's no orthodox place for his hat and options to plop his headpiece on the seat of the chair next to him. The moment is over in seconds but speaks volumes about his character.

Steve would later recycle this moment in his film *The Sand Pebbles* where he's an enlisted soldier at a fancy dinner and with food being served he doesn't know what to do with the artfully folded napkin on his plate.

Wanted Dead or Alive through the years became a breeding ground for moments Steve would later recycle in his big films. Such as his reaction to canned peaches in *Nevada Smith*, his whistle in *Never So Few*, and the early morning wake up scene in *Bullitt*. Even his raspy voice as a dying man in *Papillon* was first done in an episode of

Wanted Dead or Alive.

    The first season of *Wanted Dead or Alive* caught the attention of renowned director John Sturges. Sturges was looking to replace Sammy Davis Jr. in his upcoming big-budget World War II film *Never So Few*. He found the easygoing toughness he was looking for in Steve McQueen. After his first season of *Wanted* Steve was set to film his first ensemble picture and the beginnings of his legendary film career.

Never So Few
1959

"It had always been our plan that the road to film was through television, though at the time, no television star had ever made the transition from television to film." -Hilly Elkins

Up until this point, Steve had only had large roles in small films, here he would have a smaller role in a larger film. *Never So Few* would prove to be a great setting and a good test for Steve, as this film would appraise his potential to move from TV star to movie star. Not all television actors can become movie stars and in the 1950s' no actor had ever made the leap, studios simply stuck with what an actor had already proven to work.

One reason no actor had ever made the leap had to do with talent. In a television series, the audience has more time to become emotionally attached to the show and characters, which allows actors of lesser talent to seem better than they truly are because a caring audience will overlook their flaws. An actor can't rely on this handicap in the fast pace of movies.

The star of *Never So Few* was Frank Sinatra, which turned out to be a blessing for Steve and his career. Sinatra enjoyed Steve's completive nature and decided to take him under his wing. What added to Steve's blessing was the fact that John Sturges was only able to keep Sinatra on set from 9 am to 5 pm. Right at 5 pm, Sinatra would start walking off set to go party. He'd call out to Sturges, "Give the kid all the close-ups," as he'd leave the set even if they were in the middle of a scene.

Steve always made the most out of every opportunity and in this film he's the most memorable aspect of the whole picture. *Never So Few* is not without flaws; Sinatra seems distracted and his romance isn't believable, also

35

the jungle sets are alarmingly fake. But the flaws are overruled when McQueen comes on the screen with all his magnetism.

The first time Steve's character, Bill Ringa, appears he is driving a jeep as if he stole the government issued vehicle and he's late for a hot date. Then when he parks he takes the gum out of his mouth and sticks the pink nugget to the side of the windshield as if he's going to save the treat for later. He is absolutely bursting with personality and the camera picks up everything.

In the story, Bill Ringa is the General's personal driver and he knows his abilities as a soldier aren't being fully taken advantage of. He talks to Sinatra's character about the fighting he did growing up in the streets of New York and comments, "You know the funny part about it is since I joined the army and the war's started I've lived a comparatively sheltered life." Ringa then shows promise as a good fighter by taking out two Military Police Officers who catch him drinking. This prompts Sinatra's character, Captain Reynolds, to draft him into his front line unit which is what Ringa wants.

Those are the events of the story and different actors could go about playing the scenes differently. Most actors playing Ringa would formulate their characters objective of being drafted to the front line around getting Captain Renolds approval. But Steve has read the script and knows that in the end, no matter what tactic he personally chooses, Captain Renolds will draft him to his unit because those events are written in the script. This is where Steve shamelessly plays his movie-acting secret, the cool card. By actively not seeking the approval of Captain Renolds Steve makes the events appear as if he's the one doing them the favor by joint the unit, not the other way around as most actors would choose to portray.

Once Ringa gets to the front lines he proves that he's

the most proficient soldier and Steve is able to show this to the audience. When their unit comes under an ambush the American soldiers and their Burmese allies immediately scramble around looking for cover. Everyone except for Ringa. Steve chose to stop and assess the situation first, half-eaten watermelon still in hand, then he takes action grabbing a short range mortar that devastates the enemy while the other soldiers fire aimlessly with pistols and sub-machine guns. By Steve adding in that brief pause to assess the situation, he shows his expertise as a soldier so later when Captain Renolds gives Ringa command of the squad the audience already knows he's fully capable.

This is a strategy Steve employed throughout his career. There are lines of dialogue written into the script which sets up Ringa's leadership abilities but this was something that Steve added himself; giving Ringa more authenticity. Being able to show the audience is always more impressive than telling them. Steve knew this and he is quoted in many interviews stating how intelligent audiences are.

The New York Herald Tribune wrote in their review, "Steve McQueen looks good as a brash casual GI. He possesses that combination of smooth-rough charm that suggests star possibilities." And they were absolutely right, *Never So Few* set Steve McQueen on a path to becoming a movie star and in doing so he would become the first actor to successfully make the jump from television to the movies. But before that could happen he needed to fulfill his *Wanted Dead or Alive* contract.

Wanted: Dead or Alive seasons 2 & 3
1959-1961

"I worked hard, and if you work hard you get the goodies"
-Steve McQueen

Steve's role wasn't very big in *Never So Few* but he stole the show and showed the world he was meant for a larger stage. When he returned to the second season of *Wanted* he began doing a lot of public relations gigs. He was getting both his name and the show publicity by doing things like Bob Hope's annual Christmas show, a guest spot on the *Perry Como's Musical Hour*, an episode of *Alfred Hitchcock Presents*, and was a parade marshal in Texas as well as attended a rodeo in the lone star state. This cut into filming the second season but CBS thought the publicity would benefit them.

"When you're hot you can play it very cool." -Steve McQueen

Steve McQueen was not just a person anymore, he was a name in the entertainment industry and Steve was going to do every possible thing he could think of to make that name last forever. He rode onto the screen with much more confidence the second season with a horse that's just as ornery as ever.

The reviews for the second season were coming in and were better than the first, sighting Steve for the shows success. He used this as a new power to get more of the things he wanted to be done on set, being particularly harsh on the writer/producer. Steve started demanding rewrites and would throw out an entire script if he felt the writing wasn't good enough.

"He obviously got a bad reputation," said Steve's stunt man Loren James. "A lot of the guys didn't like him. He was so definite about what he wanted and what his character needed. He argued with writers, directors, and producers. He argued with everybody. He had a good sense, a good feeling, an intuitiveness. Plus, he'd been around. He knew life, he knew the bad part of life and the sad part. He knew all of these little things they didn't. Here's a guy from New York, never been around horses, doesn't know anything about it, and he's going to play a bounty hunter. He has a short haircut and carries a sawed-off shotgun instead of a pistol. He does everything you're not supposed to do. But he worked at his acting. He worked at cowboy moves and how they thought. He wanted to make it different because the series was different."

The result of Steve's influence is a darker second season filled with cynical women, iron-fisted men, and grim monosyllabic replies from Randall. Often in this season, Randall is vilified by entire towns, remorselessly left wounded, and even sacrificed to the bad guys. Throughout all of his hardship, Randall remains cool and collected leaving an indelible impression on the show's viewers.

Donna Redden, a fan since she was a child said, "Randall was the blueprint for what a man should possess: integrity, a sense of ethics, a moral compass that runs deep and true, a sense of fun, a romantic nature, but tough and always trustworthy. He was the man to get the job done. Steve lived this role for three years and made it so thoroughly his own that I can't think it was only the writers' words in action—'Randall' truly had to be the basic Steve."

Much of what people say about McQueen is also true for the roles he inhabited. Ben Affleck said of him, "His brand of masculinity was an unassuming, easygoing toughness that's not bullying or puffing up the chest, but rather a likable commanding of respect. Appealing, yet somewhat intimidating."

The third season saw Steve as difficult to work with and as brilliant in front of the camera as ever. Ed Admson who was the writer/producer received the brunt of Steve's force but was still able to see the genius in Steve's work, "Steve isn't argumentative arbitrarily. Nobody would know more about Josh Randall than Steve. He knows exactly what Randall would do and what he wouldn't do. That doesn't mean I like it any better, but I do have respect for Steve. And when I look at the finished product, I love him. Many times I think he's wonderful, and that's hard for me to say some days."

Steve only wanted to make as good a show as he could and he was able to recognize when he went too far, "One mistake I made was forgetting about the dignity of my directors. I'd get into a scene, and suddenly I'd be telling' the other actors how to play it. Then I'd have to go over and apologize to the director."

Hilly Elkins, "Steve was a perfectionist, but if he felt something was important, it didn't matter if it was important or not to anyone else, it was important to him. Most of his energies were focused on things that made a difference. His instinct about himself was unerring. Steve made that character in that show his own. It was his contribution that made it something other than another television show. Josh Randall was a reactor; that was Steve's greatest talent. It was body language, it was the face, it was the raised eyebrow, it was the look across the camera, and the camera loved Steve. This man with no literary, artistic background had this incredible animal instinct about himself and about what worked."

The episode titled *The Voice of Silence* most depicts Randall as a reactor as he spends the entire show babysitting a young girl who's deaf and dumb. Throughout the episode, she communicates to him by writing notes whereas Steve is able to communicate effectively by his natural reactions, which appears effortless.

40

The second season introduced Randall's traveling companion, Jason who was a young green horn deputy turned bounty hunter. Their interactions with one another brought an interesting dynamic to the show but Jason left before the season ended. The third season brought nothing new to the show and the series started losing luster with the fans as did all other TV westerns.

"The market was going in a different direction," Hilly said. "This was the early Four Star days when you had *Zane Grey Theater* and *Trackdown* and *Wanted Dead or Alive* and a whole slew of westerns on television. The mood of the American public started going away from that type of show, and it just got more expensive to produce, so after so many years, you went on to a new situation."

But in the end, CBS might be the one to blame for the shows poor ratings and ultimate cancellation after 94 episodes when they moved the show from Saturday night to Wednesday night. Neile has said about the cancellation, "While Steve was relieved to be rid of the series, he was also terribly angry that CBS had killed a good show by moving it to a bad time spot. But he needed now to try and learn new things. He had gotten all he could out of these three seasons he had spent with the series, and it was time to move onto the big screen."

During an interview, Steve was asked if he was upset the show was being canceled to which he replied, "Hell, no! I was delighted. That series was murder on me. Still, I'm grateful to ol' Josh Randall. I'll always owe him one for giving me a running start in this business. Right now, I've got a real chance to grab that brass ring, and man, you better believe I'm ready to do some grabbing'."

The Magnificent Seven
1960

"Movie acting is reacting. Silence is golden on the screen." -Steve McQueen

When John Sturges plucked Steve McQueen from television to replace Samy Davis Jr. in *Never So Few* he knew what he was doing. "When [McQueen] walked into my office, he had the same thing that you saw later in *The Magnificent Seven* and *The Great Escape*—brashness cut with insecurity. He was a bundle of contradictions. But he had an immediate scene sense."

Sturges wanted Steve back for his next big picture *The Magnificent Seven*, a Western genre remake of Akira Kurosawa's legendary film *The Seven Samurai*. There were, however, two things holding Steve back from appearing in the film as Vin Tanner. The first one was that there were only seven lines of dialogue for his character and Steve's agent Hilly Elkins wanted confirmation that this wasn't some bit part. Sturges never said he'd give Steve more lines but instead told Hilly, "I promise I'll give him the camera."

"John Sturges was one of the few men in this town whose word was as good as gold," Hilly said. And with that Steve recognized that this role could give him the stardom that he craved if only he could delay the filming of the third season of *Wanted: Dead or Alive*.

The producers of *Wanted* had no intention of delaying the production of their hit TV show and weren't about to let Steve go and make a film in Mexico that would make other people money. Hilly decided action needed to be taken and went to Steve, simply telling him, "Have an accident." Hilly later recalled, "I felt comfortable advising Steve on that level because of his racing and driving skills, and I knew he'd be careful but convincing. But I had no idea he would take it to the level that he did."

Steve and his wife were in a rented Cadillac when Steve spotted the perfect opportunity to stage his accident. He prepared his wife for what was about to happen, gave her a kiss, and stepped on the gas. Neile remembers, "It was only a matter of seconds from the moment he stepped on the gas to going over an island and onto the wall. The hotel doorman was aghast. It was the last thing he had ever expected to see, right there in front of him! He ran to us to see if we were all right and the pandemonium that ensued was exactly what we had hoped for."

Days later when the head of Four Star Productions saw Steve in a neck brace he knew he had no choice to but to delay production for a few months, which was just long enough for Steve to go off with Sturges and make *The Magnificent Seven*.

For *The Magnificent Seven*, John Sturges put together a who's who of future movie stars. He cast Steve McQueen, Eli Wallach, James Coburn, Robert Vaughn, Charles Bronson, Brad Dexter, and 'The European Sensation' Horst Buchholz. Only one of the actors cast was an established movie star at the time and that was Yul Brynner who had just won an Academy Award for his role in *The King and I*.

Before filming began Sturges had a tactic he enjoyed using to help get on the same page as his actors. He took his cast to Western Costume and would layout hats, shirts, boots, holsters, and guns on tables and racks. Then the actors would go through the thousands of wardrobe possibilities and pick out what they felt was right for their character. The resulting outfits were as unique as they were.

Robert Reyla said, "[Sturges] enjoyed so much seeing what he was imagining come to life on somebody and see what they looked like and say no that hat's not right and everything and everybody just enjoyed it they had a good time." Robert Vaughn, one of the actors noted his experience, "I just picked out whatever I wanted to wear and that's what people have talked about for years because my costume was so unlike the others. I guess I was kind of a dandy."

Yul Brynner as the leader of the seven men wore black boots, black pants, a black holster, black shirt, and a black hat to cover his shining bald head. Steve played his second in command and in contrast chose lighter colors; light brown leather boots and belts, blue jeans covered in stove pipe chaps, a soft colored shirt which he usually kept only half way buttoned up to show off his gold medallion necklace that he owned personally and wore in many of his films. He also wore a blue handkerchief around his neck which made his blue eyes stand out that much more.

Steve's holster/revolver combination was an interesting choice as his gun has a 7 1/2 inch barrel where as his holster was made for a gun with only a 5 1/2 inch barrel. This results in two inches of the silver gun barrel to be exposed out the bottom of the holster, which would catch the sunlight and shimmer as he walked. Every choice he made was to be visually cinematic and to attract the attention of the audience.

The wardrobe fittings were among the first days of all of the actors getting together and there were already signs of the competition to come. Reyla noted, "Those rooms were always mirrored and I was amused to see that they were all looking at each other just like John was looking at them. It was as if they were saying to themselves 'I want a hat like his hat' or 'I want spurs bigger than his spurs,' which in the right spirit and under a good director, is healthy competition to have on a set."

John Sturges was a director who knew what he wanted. He would daydream about a film until he knew exactly what he wanted to shoot then he'd storyboard his daydream shot for shot. Sturges would hang up the storyboards all over his office. Coburn got to look at them when he went in to meet Sturges for the first time and said after filming that everything was shot exactly as the storyboard pictured it. His storyboards were for setting up a scene cinematically but Coburn noted, "You were free within that form to do whatever you wanted to do and that's what he counted on it, he hired you for what you could bring to put in that square." In fact, throughout the entire film, Sturges only required Coburn to do one specific thing on camera. At the railhead, Sturges wanted a shot of Coburn pushing his hat up with one finger to reveal his eyes then look over to another actor, that was all.

On *Never So Few,* Sturges nurtured Steve as the man with the quiet laid back strength and once that was established he trusted Steve within that persona in all their films together. Robert Vaughn said, "As far as directing the actors, John seldom said a word to anyone. I guess once he got McQueen and Brynner, he figured they knew what they were doing. The only person John spoke to with any regularity was Charles Lang, the cinematographer. They'd set up the scene photographically, do the master shot until they got what they wanted, and then go in close." Eli Wallach loved the freedom of Sturges style of directing and said, "What I liked as an actor was that he never imposed his choice on the actor. If he liked what was done we moved on to the next scene. If he didn't like it he'd say, 'Well let's try it again.'"

"The basic thing was that Sturges was able to mix all these diverse characters and personalities and from that develop a kind of competitiveness but at the same time a likeability between all of us." -Brad Dexter.

With the exception of Eli, every actor saw himself as the next big movie star and the one who would overthrow Yul's kingdom. This became apparent during the very first scene Sturges shot. Eli was standing by the camera watching those first few moments unfold, "Each one of them did something as they passed the camera so that you would remember them. I was very amused by it all."

Robbert Relyea remembers vividly the circus that ensued. "There were three or four rehearsals, which were six or seven people in a row on horseback just riding by and looking about from side to side. But when film was going through the camera Steve swung out of the saddle with his hat, scooped up water from the stream and doused it on himself. Next, I think was Charlie Bronson who unbuttoned his shirt, stretched, turned his bandana around. Then came Brad Dexter who did 3 acts of *Hamlet*! And poor Yul didn't know what was going on behind him while everybody was trying to stake their ground and to [say] 'this is going to be my picture, I have six supporting cast.' And [John Sturges] the cigarette hanging from his mouth never said cut or anything else, it's just his eyes got wider and he turned and looked at me and what he was saying was, 'Can you believe that we're gonna go on for six or eight weeks with these guys."

Sturges called these attention-getting antics "catching flies" and they would become a major staple in each of the actor's arsenal of scene-stealing tactics. According to Coburn, Yul never expected competition for screen time from his fellow actors because he saw himself as King. Steve noted how he was supposed to act when working with the King and how he responded to that, "When you work in a scene with Yul, you're supposed to stand perfectly still ten feet away. I don't work that way. So I protected myself."

The way Steve protected himself was by lessening Yul's presence on screen. One day Yul went up to Steve, who was known as having an extraordinary draw to ask him to teach him how to properly draw his revolver from his holster. "Steve's main aim was to promote Steve McQueen," Coburn said. "Steve was prepared in all of his roles. He had a great reputation for his draw. Very quick. It really worked for him. I remember Yul saying, 'I don't know what to do with my gun.' And Steve gave him an ordinary move to draw the pistol and put it back in the holster. It's been done a thousand times over and Yul used it. So Steve was very proud that he conned Yul into a simple move, while he did this fancy thing with his pistol."

When Yul saw that he wasn't going to match Steve's ability with a revolver he changed tactics. Steve realized, "He wanted me to use a rifle in the film so that I wouldn't outdraw him, but I wouldn't have that. We were shooting the first battle sequences. I got three shots out before he even had his gun out of his holster."

Another exchange between Steve and Yul was noticed by Steve's manager Hilly Elkins, "Steve and Yul Brynner weren't that tall. In one of their scenes, Brynner built himself a little mound of dirt to stand on to appear taller. Steve is circling saying his lines. Every time he passes Yul, he kicks away at the dirt pile Yul is standing on, so throughout the scene, you see Yul is getting smaller and smaller. By the end of the scene, Yul is standing in a hole!"

Getting the better of Yul was a big deal to Steve. "He was paranoid about Yul Brynner, who was the star of the picture," said Robert Vaughn. "One time he said to me, 'Did you see how big Brynner's horse is?' I said, 'No, as a matter of fact, they're calling my horse 'Elefante.' I think my horse is bigger than his.' He said, 'No, no, Brynner's horse is a lot bigger!' He was angry about this. Shortly after that, he came to me to talk about Brynner having a white handled gun or something, which he hadn't noticed. He thought it might take attention away from him. He plotted every day to better Yul Brynner."

47

Executive producer Walter Mirisch said, "Yul was then a very big star and knew he was the star of the film. Yul was not a man lacking in self-confidence and was not shaken by Steve's presence, or anyone else's. From where I was standing, he got along okay with Steve, who treated him with respect most of the time. I was along with the two of them many times and their relationship was fine; Steve was the young, aspiring actor who was doing everything he could to make his part better and be noticed, while Yul always knew that he had the commanding role - he was a thorough professional."

The competitiveness didn't carry off the set and Yul's wife, who he married during production, has said that all the cast absolutely loved playing cowboys practicing with the guns and riding horses "all they wanted to do were cowboy movies."

Relyea said of Steve and Yul, "I think you'd be able to tell if there was serious friction between them. They couldn't play scenes alone together that well if they were at each others throat - it would show. Keen and on their toes — yes, competitive — yes, but they were never growling. Those two guys understood each other."

The main thing Steve understood was that he was the star when the cameras were rolling and he was going to make sure the audience never took their eyes off of him, he was going to make this his breakout role. "Steve wasn't what you would call a giving guy," said James Coburn. "He had a lot of power and presence. He loved to play. It was in his nature. An abandoned child always tests everything, and he tested Yul." John Sturges compared them this way, "They're dissimilar characters. Yul was like a rock, while Steve was volatile." The first scene of them together in the film is a ride on a stagecoach to deliver an Indian corps to the gravesite atop of Boot Hill. Yul grabs the reins while Steve rides shotgun with a shotgun.

With all his subtle elegance Yul preps a cigar while his head is on a swivel looking out for danger. He might as well been doing nothing as Steve, on the other hand, isn't so subdued. Steve grabs two shotgun shells and one at a time shakes them close to his ear listening to the rattle of the shot before putting them into the loading breach of his "skater gun." Then with a strong flick of the wrist, he snaps the barrels to the receiver. Now that the gun is loaded Steve holds his hat up to the sky shading his eyes to see danger more comfortably, he puts the hat back on his head and cocks each of the individual barrels before looking over to Yul. McQueen's actions are much more grandiose and even though Yul is the star of the film and is the focal point of the camera, all eyes are on Steve. "It was a wonderful competitive moment," Eli said. "Sturges loved the competition and never chastised his actors for it."

A cowboy's hat say's a lot about the cowboy. Eli Wallach and Steve McQueen took great care in choosing their hats but they weren't just statement pieces or for shading their eyes from the sun. As actors, Eli and Steve chose their hats for specific reasons related to acting.

Eli Wallach had a huge authentic black sombrero made for him in Mexico. His plan was that in close up shots, and even some mid shots, his hat was big enough to block out the entire background and eliminate any distractions from his face and thus his performance. Steve's hat was also part of his performance.

He had picked out a light tan colored cowboy hat who's color changed the more he sweat. The brim was curled up on the sides so much that any real cowboy would see the hat is useless because of how little shade the brim provided. But the curled brim did allow the camera full access to his face from any angle, which was more important than being true to life in this case.

Steve's hat became a very intimate part of his fly catching antics as well. In total Steve touched or fiddled with his hat 20 different times in the final cut of the film and 14 of those were when Yul was also in the frame. Yul took this as Steve's way of specifically trying to steal attention away from Yul. Most commonly Steve would be behind Yul in the background of a shot fanning himself with his hat while Yul stood still engaged in conversation and unaware of what was going on behind him. In other scenes, Steve and Yul would be having a conversation together and Steve would take his hat off or pick dirt out of the brim as he pondered something. Steve also commonly took his hat off when entering a building and he'd put his hat back on when he exited.

Whether or not Steve was deliberately trying to scene steal with his hat would often indicate something about what he was going through. Fanning himself in the hot desert of Mexico makes sense and fiddling with a hat as a social tick or when someone's pondering something is reasonable. The real genius was in the fact that all his fly catching were biased in the authenticity of living in the moment. Steve's hat, as well as every article of his clothing, was an extension of his character, not just outer clothing. Sturges explains, "When Steve pushed his hat back on his head, it was his response to a thing but Yul was convinced that Steve was scene-stealing, fussing around with his hat behind his close-up." Yul even had a guy on set who's sole purpose was to tell him if Steve was playing with his hat during their scenes together.

John Sturges chose to allow the fly catching to continue throughout the film and what impressed actor Brad Dexter was that Sturges "was able to mix all these diverse characters and personalities and from that develop a kind of competitiveness but at the same time a like-ability between all of us." The competitiveness wasn't carried over into everyone's downtime unless they were playing a friendly game of poker. A few of the guys would even get together and go into town to drink and check out the local

Mexican señoritas. But, as Yul's wife noted, above all the cast absolutely loved playing cowboys and they would practice with the guns and go horseback riding for hours. Brad Dexter said, "I had more fun on that picture than any picture I ever made,"

The Magnificent Seven has gone on to be an iconic film and one of the most played movies on television. After the film was released Sturges was fortunate enough to meet Akira Kurosawa who gave him a samurai sword as a gift telling him he loved The Magnificent Seven. Sturges considered this his proudest moment of his professional career.

Steve, however, was the real winner of the film proving how far a little cunning can get a relentless man. "That movie made Steve a star because Steve kissed ass, talked to Sturges, did things his way. He didn't want to be Josh Randall the rest of his life. And Steve became bigger than all of them," said Phil Parslow. James Coburn who went on to have a very successful career as an actor laughed as he told Steve years after making the film "We were so busy hating you that you stole the movie. You were the smart guy. We were dumb."

Hell Is For Heroes & The War Lover
1962

"I always try to immerse myself in the role I'm playing." - Steve McQueen

As if to show the world he was capable of heavy dramatic acting Steve set out to play a character incredibly rough and world-weary. So much so that director Stanley Kubrick was prompted to send Steve a letter. In which he wrote, "It's the most perceptive and realistic performance of any soldier in any war film I have seen." And Kubrick is one who would know having made *Paths to Glory* and later the Vietnam War film *Full Metal Jacket*.

Hell Is For Heroes is about a small squad that's forced to hold a segment of the Siegfried line against overwhelming Nazi forces. Steve was playing the lead role of Reese, a battle-hardened soldier who had recently been demoted to Private, assumably for disobeying orders that would have pointlessly killed American lives.

Steve took an approach to this film that he never attempted before. He was going to allow his on-camera character dictate how he behaved off camera. Steve was mindful of his cast mates and as a curtsy let them know early on, "Man, I like you guys. But I'm not supposed to like you in the movie, so I've got to live apart from you guys and not have anything to do with you during the shoot." Steve was very respectful of his fellow actors throughout this film and he didn't indulge in any of the fly catching he used so readily on *The Magnificent Seven*.

Sonny West who worked on the film said, "McQueen was definitive in his approach to acting, which made it interesting to watch him work. He was intense, a loner, and gave off a vibe that made it obvious that unless he expressly invited you to speak to him, you shouldn't.

When McQueen wasn't shooting a scene, he pumped weights, often joined by James Coburn, with the grim intensity of someone trying to work off a lot of pent-up tension."

There were some tribulations Steve would have to go through in making this film. For one, the props were incredibly cheap and Steve's gun was constantly malfunctioning. Near the end of the film, there was an unscripted malfunction when his M3 Grease Gun jams, Steve appropriately throws the gun down out of disgust and continues the scene.

But the biggest headache Steve had to endure were the threats of Paramount's executives who wanted to shut down production after the film had gone a million dollars over budget. Nowadays with films costing in the hundreds of millions this sum of money isn't that big of a deal but back in 1962 this was a big deal. Especially when the original budget was only $900,000. And as the legend goes the Paramount executives came down to set one day to officially close down production. Steve was tipped off and met them on the set drawing a line in the dirt and declaring, "Anyone who steps over that lines gets the shit knocked out of him." After that, the executives left and never threatened the film again.

Steve was also unhappy with an aspect of the script. Originally the film was to feature much more of the ensemble cast but Steve saw the film more about one person. The film was rewritten to focus more heavily on Steve's character, which worked well as many of the other actors develop cliché characters or are simply poor actors. Exercising his power to change the script was something he'd do a lot more in his next ensemble film, *The Great Escape*.

Right after *Hell Is For Heroes* Steve filmed *The War*

Lover where he plays, Buzz Rickson, a character who has elements that are the complete opposite of Reese. "A kind of schizophrenic," Steve himself said, "He revels in war and destruction. He lives for killing." The common thread between these two charters is Steve McQueen's personal essence; they're all animals of instinct, tough, and determined men who are willing to make the tough decisions that no one else will. And for these two films, there's an underlying feeling that neither of them could survive in a world without war, Reese because he's too damaged and Rickson because he'd miss the thrill too much.

Like he did in *Hell Is For Heroes*, Steve separated himself from the rest of the cast and crew saying at the time, "I have to stay in character." However, after filming Steve had a change of heart about how he played his character, "I got too involved with him. By the time I got home at night after a days work, I'm physically and mentally exhausted."

These two films are the only accounts of Steve staying in character throughout production. In all his other films he doesn't burden himself with this technique and instead chooses to save that energy for when the camera is rolling. And for all the effort put into staying in character, there doesn't seem to be any advantage in the final product. His acting even seems a little stiff in both films; although, this could have something to do with the direction he was given by the directors.

The Great Escape
1963

"If they were making a movie of my life that's what they'd call it, *The Great Escape*." -Steve McQueen

Steve's next movie would be another ensemble film and another collaboration between him and director John Sturges. *The Great Escape* was based on the real-life tale of allied prisoners of war in a Nazi prison camp. "It was about why our side won," said Sturges. "Here were these guys who had never seen each other in their lives, all different nationalities, who formed an organization to escape. They're a microcosm of the Allies, men who voluntary formed the most professional army ever put together to wipe out the Nazis. I saw it as a movie about this uncontrolled, individualistic, do-it-your-way form of life —our way of life—which defeated those dictatorial sons-a-bitches."

Of all the actors in Hollywood, there was one above the others that fit that description. Steve McQueen played the ill-mannered American pilot Hiltz, Captain Hiltz. He would have his first top billing and yet when he got to Germany for filming his role had yet to be fully developed in the script. He was going to have to fight and stick to his guns to make this a career defining role.

All the actors playing leading roles, save for Steve, had a particular job to do in helping everyone escape the prison camp. Richard Attenborough played 'Big X', the leader of X-Organization, Charles Bronson was the 'Tunnel King', James Coburn was 'The Manufacturer,' and James Garner was 'The Scrounger.' There were also actors who played 'SBO' (Senior British Officer), 'Forger,' 'Surveyor,' 'Intelligence,' 'Dispersal,' and more yet Steve didn't have that clear identifying function within the team and this troubled him.

As each of the other actors' roles was based on a specific person who had a specific job within the organization each actor playing them had a specific job. Steve's role, on the other hand, was based on a combination of a number of soldiers at the camp so he didn't have a clear and specific job that made him memorable. "Where's my thing?" Steve would ask.

"He had to find his niche. Steve didn't feel he had his thing," Robert Relyea said. "Charlie Bronson had his shovel and his pick as 'The Tunnel King'; Jim Garner could work on his part as 'The Scrounger', but Steve didn't have anything and he felt he couldn't work without a defined character to play."

And without a defined character to play Steve's wife knew, "The part of Virgil Hilts was still ambiguous. Hilts had no real personality. He was bland and he was boring. Steve knew that, given this cast, unless he came up with something interesting for this role he would blend in with the scenery. He had absolutely no intention of letting that happen."

John Sturges was very patient with Steve as he struggled to find a way to make Hilts memorable. "He was groping around, ad-libbing, trying to figure out how he could make the switch from loner to a member of the 'X' team. I couldn't get Steve to realize that that was his part, the loner. He kept getting upset because he wasn't involved with the mechanism of the escape." But even loners need to have a purpose and Steve fought with Sturges as he was unable to articulate exactly what he felt his role and the story needed.

The film had been in production and filming for weeks but Steve refused to step foot in front of the camera until his role in the film was fixed. Steve was ready to walk off the picture and Sturges was ready to fire him, "I'm getting tired of arguing with you. If you don't like this part, to hell with it. We'll pay you off, and I'll shift to Jim Garner." The thought of his scenes going to his TV rival James Garner was enough to make Steve reassess his tactics and calm down.

John Leyton who played Willie noted, "I saw Steve a few times at one of these restaurants and he would be in pretty deep conversation with John Sturges, just the two of them. The rest of us were out socializing and having a drink in our own groups, but Steve was still 'at work'. It soon became known that Steve had a problem with his role and he did what he could to change it. To Steve's credit, he never mentioned it once to me that he was unhappy with his role. And as far as I know, he never mentioned it to anybody else. Other people may have made a song and dance out of it. So in that respect, he was very professional and only aired his opinions to the director and producers."

Production continued to film but Steve didn't appear in a single foot of film for the first six weeks of filming. But because no one was sure if Steve would be in the film or not, scenes were shot not even mentioning his character.

James Garner and James Coburn spent two hours one night talking to Steve before they realized what Steve's dilemma was, "Steve wanted to be the hero, but he didn't want to do anything physically heroic." In a last attempt to appease Steve the Oscar-nominated writer Ivan Moffat was flown in to do script rewrites.

Ivan Moffat's script changes were able to get to the heart of what Steve had difficulty putting into words and his rewrites produced Steve's most iconic moments of the film. With Steve's character Hilts missing from 6 weeks of shooting Ivan Moffat had the challenging task of not only making Steve happy but also in showing why Hilts was absent from the scenes already shot. This produced several solo scenes of Hilts that made him stand apart from the rest of the cast.

Ivan was able to incorporate Steve's baseball and

catchers mitt in both the testing of the blind spots in the perimeter fences and in his time spent in solitary confinement known as "The Cooler." Bouncing a baseball off a wall and catching the ball upon the return was something he did a lot by himself at the Boys Republic.

Playing catch with himself in the film is an independent activity as taught by Sanford Meisner. Steve engages all of his focus into this simple action as if he said to himself, "I'm going to do this perfectly or die trying." The determination to which he brings this activity is what makes the simple scene in the cooler so compelling and memorable. The audience links his determination in the action to his resistance to Nazi oppression.

"I spent a whole day in that cell with Steve when he wasn't working, just practicing his method, throwing that baseball," said Relyea. "It became a symbol that he was thinking once again at how he would try to escape next time." Steve knew what the story and his role needed, if he had thrown the ball casually as if to simply pass time, as most actors would have done, then these scenes would hold no value and would have been forgotten.

Moffat was also able to give the role the type heroism Steve desired by making Hilts the character who volunteers to escape, retrieve the unknown information, then be captured again. Hilts's efforts get him thrown into the cooler and his sacrifice is what gives him purpose within the X-Organization. More importantly to Steve, this sacrifice makes him memorable as 'The Cooler King.'

"That was all written in just to buttress up Steve's role," producer Walter Mirisch said. "That was done to show Steve's self-sacrifice. It added footage to an already long film, which was something John Sturges and I were concerned about. But as often happens when making movies, after a while, we began to like it and thought it was a real good idea, which we should have thought of earlier! Despite all the troubles, I really don't think Steve was ever close to quitting. He liked being in the picture; he had a good instinct for it and knew this was going to be a successful picture. Steve had great confidence in it and of course, he was right because it is certainly one of the best pictures of his life."

Relyea noted that "Once those additions to his part were made, Steve really flushed it out and went to work. He thought all the time and he often said: 'I shouldn't be comfortable when I'm working because that's not when I do my best.' Eventually, he would become comfortable when he had found the tools to work with, like the motorcycle chase."

Steve only accepted the role of Capt. Hilts on the condition that he got to show off his motorcycle skills and Ivan was able to put the motorcycle chase into the script. From the moment Steve first steals the German motorcycle he displays his expert riding skills. So by the end of the case when the daring jump over the fence comes the audiences believe that's Steve flying through the air and not a stunt double (even if that was a double) because he has already proven with his skills that he would have been capable of doing the jump.

Later on once Steve finally crashes into the barbed-wire fence and he knows he's going to be captured he looks down at the bike and gives his friend a little pat. Without any words, he displays humility to an inanimate object giving all the more meaning to the climactic chase.

Steve's and Ivan's contributions are what make the film so memorable and iconic. John Sturges believed in McQueen enough to put up with all of his demands and antics, he said, "When you find somebody with that kind of talent, you use him. Steve is unique. The way Cary Grant is unique, or Spencer Tracy or Marlon Brando. There's something bubbling inside of him; he's got a quality of excitement that he brings to everything he does. Like most good actors, he likes and 'attitude'—he likes to know where he stands in relation to the action of a scene, rather than just come on and act—then he goes from there. Steve has a great interest in people. Watch him as he sits there and listens, hunching himself up. That's why you can't take your eyes off him on screen. He's alive!"

There's an element of danger that Steve exudes and is part of what makes him so magnetic on the screen but his magnetism is unavailing without his authenticity. His authenticity comes from adapting and injecting his physicality into his roles. The riding he does in the film has validity because he's a passionate motorcycle racer. His expertise in the handling and operating firearms comes from his service in the Marines where he was given sharp shooter status with both the M1 Garand and the 1911 Colt 45. In addition, he stipulated that gym equipment be installed at all filming locations over two weeks long and he worked out for two hours a day for the reason of adding credibility to his action scenes.

But the most important aspect of Steve bringing authenticity to his work was in using his own personality to beef up the believability of his role. James Coburn noticed, "The British would always base their character on what the character would do, whereas Steve would base his character on what Steve McQueen would do. And, strangely enough, it worked for him. That personality, that theme is what he created and everybody in the theater wanted to see it."

Finding moments in Steve's acting where he is "play acting" is not easy because more often than not he plants his feet, looks the other person square in the face, and tells his truth. This produces moments of absolute sincerity as to who he is as a person. His manager Hilly noticed the unrefined vulnerability that laid within his manly exterior when he said, "There was a raw vulnerability underneath all that bravado. I mean he was a man's, man. He could set the feminist cause back a hundred and fifty years by just saying, 'Hello'. But that was all real but underneath that was a very insecure guy who would never open that up except on camera when it suited him."

Everything Steve did on film lived inside him and part of the McQueen magic was when he opened up to the camera so that the audience would see that truth living inside of him. "He was forever fighting to cut lines because he knew, better than anyone, that one telling look is worth any amount of dialogue," said Sir Richard Attenborough. And because Steve was so brazen about laying himself bare in his onscreen personality Hilly noted, "He would get more out of a 'Yep' than most people get out of a monologue."

Steve's judgment in accordance with his camera technique also aided him when working with other actors. Coburn said, "Steve liked to watch the scene being rehearsed and watch how others would act so he would know all the boundaries to watch out for." Not only did he not want to be upstaged or out acted but also he would look for opportunities to stand out amongst the other actors. Steve could stand out by simple blocking, through action, stillness, fly-catching, and by looking for the unexpected acting choice. Sir Richard Attenborough called Steve, "One of the best screen actors of all time."

"It was a great chance for Steve to show his qualities, even more so than *The Magnificent Seven*," said Relyea. "After this picture, the path was open for him because the industry and the public recognized him for what he was— a star."

The Great Escape was a mega hit around the world and McQueen had now achieved the level of commercial success he had always known he would reach. He was providing for his growing family, now with two children and showing the world that this once unloved kid was worth something. Steve's success was attained not by perfecting an act or milking a genera but by making the best of every situation. "It didn't cause other people happiness, but it did cause him to be a star, so you can't fault that," Coburn said. "He was a very complicated, complex guy, yet he was very simple. Very simple and straightforward. He was selfish, but I don't think he thought he was being selfish. I thought he was doing everything for the good of him. That's not selfish, but self-protective. I think that stems from being an abandoned child. It was all a test. A psychological thing.

The role in *The Great Escape* wasn't originally built around him. He had to develop it. He wanted that separation from the other men. He was in the cell and always had to be brought in as a separate prisoner. He was always an individual, which was very clever of him."

The Great Escape was Steve's vehicle to movie stardom and he himself made this possible. Attenborough summed up Steve's presence on set and in the picture, "Steve was very professional. If the script was bad, which it was in the first draft of *The Great Escape*, then yes he put up a fuss. He was a perfectionist in every sense of the word. All those rumors about his being hard to get along with are scandalously untrue. I can remember rehearsing with him for weeks because we had a lot of scenes together. Not one incident of ugly behavior sticks out in my mind. I admired his integrity.

He had that aura of mystique that at any time he was going to blow up into a thousand pieces. He was available emotionally. There were no pretenses. He gave you that feeling that if you were to meet him on the street, he would be totally approachable. He also had that slight wickedness that came across on the screen."

For his portrayal of Captain Hiltz, Steve won best actor at the Moscow international film festival. But perhaps most importantly, as James Coburn noted, "Steve's performance was perfect in the film. He represented everything about the indomitable spirit these guys had."

Love With The Proper Stranger
1963

"They call me a chauvinist pig. I am... and I don't give a damn!" - Steve McQueen

After becoming known world wide as an action star his next goal was to become an A-list actor and Steve couldn't do that without being a romantic leading man. He set out to do just that in his next film *Love With The Proper Stranger*. Steve is no prince charming but he brings his own personal touches to the romantic male lead and in doing so he received a Golden Globe nomination for his performance of Rocky, a man with hidden virtues. In return, his leading lady Natalie Wood received an Academy Award nomination for her performance of Angie, a confident and modern woman.

Steve in this film is great because he is specific in every single acting choice that he makes and he has an opinion expressed at every moment. But what made this performance special for Steve is the fact that Rocky is the first three-dimensional character he ever put together. As a multifaceted individual on the screen Steve allows the audience to see all the different shades of his personality, the movements of his soul, and his idiosyncrasies.

Up until this film, all of Steve's on screen character choices came from a central desire. For instance, in *The War Lover*, all of the choices he made came from the instant gratification he gets from war and stealing women. The romance between Rocky and Angie however, provided Steve a broad range of specifics to play with. Steve's choices early on in the story make Rocky charming but in an unflattering way. As the story progress and the relationship between the two deepens Steve is able to open up and communicate the complex emotions that lie within his character.

In the abortion scene, Rocky barges in to stop the

63

procedure with a macho visceral energy that stems from his sweet, compassionate, and protective sides. In this moment he holds her and is just as vulnerable as she is. Many actors think of creating a character as having a persona but as Sanford Meisner said, "Character comes from how you feel about something." Film and television characters were described by David Mamet as illusions that are created when the courage of the actor is combined with the scripted lines of dialogue. When Steve barged into that room he was doing so with his own courage and when an actor has character his work will have character.

Love With The Proper Stranger made McQueen appeal to a whole new demographic. His wife said of this film, "It showed all the aspects that made him really appeal to women so much because it showed this macho man who dared to be vulnerable." Steve was winning over the hearts of women around the world and he was doing this the same way he won over his wife. He was himself and for the women of the world, he allowed the camera complete access to himself in this film.

Steve's performance is special for another reason because this film is so different from anyone he had been in before. He was always sure to bring authenticity to his films through the action sequences and there are none in this film. Instead, the film is full of dialogue, something that had always been a hindrance to Steve. Here he stood toe to toe with Natalie Wood through all the emotional drama. He lives truthfully under the given imaginary circumstances as well as listens and answers with his acting partner, which produces beautiful intimate moments. Steve gets genuinely irritable when Natalie plays with him by pushing his buttons and he shows both anger and regret when he upsets her.

Steve's first role as a romantic leading man in *Love With The Proper Stranger* was enlightening. *Films and*

Filming wrote "Steve McQueen contributes a quieter, stronger performance, quite free of his easy-going personal mannerisms. It is a study in boyish confusion, a mixture of defiant courage and inner fear, that is put across without tricks and is perhaps the best study of this kind of character that Hollywood has yet given us."

Steve was nominated for a Golden Globe award for Best Motion Picture Actor but his acting was to be overshadowed. Natalie Wood received a Golden Globe nomination as well as an Academy Award nomination for Best Actress in a Leading Role. She also received 2nd place at the Laurel Awards for Top Female Dramatic Performance and won the Best Actress award at the Mar del Plata Film Festival.

Overcoming limitations and impediments.

"I believe in me. I'm a little screwed up but I'm beautiful." - Steve McQueen

In a 2014 poll taken, 82% of actors that were questioned defined that the central problem they face in acting is, "Themselves." An actor's truth comes from within. Their character, self-identity, self-worth, their past, as well as their immediate circumstances all come together to form an actor's truth. And 82% of actors defined this as a problem they must overcome.

Successful actors like Steve McQueen don't view themselves as a problem; instead, they view themselves as the key to their success. Steve's loss of hearing in one ear, his speech impediment, his 9th-grade education, and his dyslexia were all overcome because they were used to his advantage.

His loss of hearing made him a man who listened with the intent to understand rather than most people who listen with the intent to reply. His speech impediment was brought on by scar tissue on the inside of his lip. He coped with this by avoiding long words and combining that with his limited education he opted for speech that anyone could understand making him the everyman.

Steve even utilized his dyslexia, a learning disability that in part makes memorizing difficult. To overcome this he adopted the tactic of cutting his lines to the bare minimum, replacing the dialogue with subtext making him someone who could win an argument through body language alone.

Steve even took this approach of utilizing his disadvantages to his film choices, "I have to be careful because I'm a limited actor. I mean, my range isn't very great. There's a whole lot of stuff I can't do, so I have to find character and situation that feel right. Even then, when I've got something that fits, it's a hell of a lot of work." By staying within his range he was able to make his work more personal.

Steve often contrasted himself to Laurence Olivier in that he wasn't the type of actor to put on a fake nose and transform himself into a different character. Instead, he constantly tried to bring his roles closer to home believing that his personal character, his distinctive mental and moral qualities, was more valuable to the story than anything he could falsify.

When Steve was first training in New York his wife Neile said, "Technique, at this point, meant to Steve feeling comfortable with the author's words and feeling comfortable with his body on stage." He was able to look at every aspect of himself as an effective part of his brand as an actor. His wife went onto say, "Later on, as a movie star, he would conclude that his personality, projected onto the screen was the most important element in his acting technique."

Because Steve infused so much of himself into his roles he is accused of not acting at all. Barbra Leigh explains. "His power came from his facial expressions and his subtle body movements. Only the camera could capture the reality of his work. I remember watching Steve during the filming of the movie and thinking he wasn't acting. But, he most certainly was. Later when I saw the completed scenes I realized that he was a master of his craft."

67

The Cincinnati Kid
1965

"Steve comes out of the tradition of Gable, Bogie, and Cagney, and even me - but he's added his own dimension. He is a stunner, and who knows what glory the future holds? But surely he is already an honorable member of the company of players." -Edward G. Robinson

In *The Cincinnati Kid*, Steve was able to follow in the footsteps of two of his all time favorite actors, Humphrey Bogart and James Cagney. Steve's role of Eric Stoner, aka 'The Kid' required street smarts, a good bad guy feel, and someone who's just as harsh as the world around him; Steve McQueen was that guy. His wife said when they were dating he never missed a Bogart or Cagney movie and here was his chance to channel those shared natures into a role either men would have been proud to play.

The Cincinnati Kid is a film about a poker game between the seasoned veteran and the up and coming young challenger. Eric Stoner was a perfect part for Steve as he's a street kid with more determination than smarts trying to break rank and move up in the world. Steve was originally attracted to the role because of the chance to act with the legendary Spencer Tracy who would play the films poker veteran.

When Steve agreed to the project there wasn't even a script but Steve wasn't worried about that. Steve said, "I know things are still up in the air, but I'm cool about everything. But just tell your writer, 'I'm better walking than I am talking." His only other stipulation was that a fight scene had to be written into the script as there are certain things audiences expect from a Steve McQueen film and a physical confrontation is one of them.

Preproduction was an eventful period with Spencer

Tracy leaving the project for health reasons and replaced by another acting legend Edward G. Robinson. Also, the wild card director Sam Peckinpah was fired and replaced by Norman Jewison. The film's shooting was further delayed when Norman wanted three weeks to rework the script to his liking.

Norman Jewison said, "When I took on the task of directing this film, there were many people who felt that a card game was death, that there was no way that you could make a film about a card game because it was just so totally uncinematic." He believed that in order to make a film about a card game work the audience had to be invested in the characters so lots of time and direction would be spent to get the audience involved in the game. "For me, the movie was about winning and losing." Norman said, "Winning is more important in the U.S. than in any other country in the world." Norman went on to say, "America has an image of the winner. He looks just like Steve McQueen."

During these delays, Steve's public relations man, Dave Resnick, knew of Steve's restlessness and said to MGM, "Just give him some money, let him go to Vegas, get the feel of this gambling thing while you guys get the picture going." The studio executives listened and gave Steve an all expenses paid trip to Las Vegas and $25,000 to gamble with on the poker tables. Steve wasn't new to poker as he played to supplement his income during his time training with Sanford Meisner. But the studio didn't know that and wanted to give Steve the sense of what playing high stakes poker is like. And the two week Vegas trip expenses were written off as "acting preparation." MGM even hired card player and magician Jay Ose as a technical advisor to help Steve and the other cast members with the intricacies of professional poker playing.

Getting a sense of high stakes poker is only preparation for one aspect of Steve's role. Apart from preparing for his specific role, film making is technically challenging for an actor. An actor must memorize pages of dialogue in advance then is often given new lines the day of shooting. When acting the actor must hit all their marks precisely as to be lit properly, stay within camera frame, and stay within focus. Also, a shot can be ruined simply by the actor bumping into the furniture and every mistake wastes time and money. In addition, the actor must become accustomed to shooting a story out of order and still hit all the emotional truths while he/she must also be fluent in the technique of acting for a camera. Not to mention the pressure of knowing a films success often rests on the shoulders of the lead actor's performance and the courage involved with laying one's soul bare for the camera in front of 50 burly crewmen who want to hurry and get the shot so they can go to lunch.

When Steve returned from his Vegas trip he was unprepared for shooting to begin as the gravity of his role in the film was dawning upon him. His costar Karl Malden said, "Steve McQueen realized he had a big challenge when he did *The Cincinnati Kid*. I have a feeling that he felt he had got into the big league." After Steve's recent successes he took time off from acting to be with his family and as a result he found returning to work challenging.

Steve said, "I'd been away from the camera for a year and the depth I was trying for in this role just wasn't coming for me. For the first three days on the set, I felt like I'd never acted before in my life. Then things got better. I loosened up and began to get my juice back." His wife also remembers this time in her memoirs, "After so much time away from acting, he found the first days of filming rather unnerving. He felt like an amateur in front of the cameras. He had sleepless nights and days of disorientation. We spent hours going over his lines. But with Norman's sure and steady guidance, it didn't take long for him once again to feel secure."

One part of Steve's early problems in the film came from not fully trusting his director. Norman had been hired while Steve was on his Vegas trip so they didn't get to meet and establish a relationship until they were on set. Steve showed on *Wanted: Dead or Alive* that if he didn't respect a director he would become difficult to work with. He had always respected and gotten along with John Sturges and later in his career Henry Hathaway because Steve looked up to them as father figures. Norman, however; was only five years older than Steve so looking at him as a father figure would have been a stretch.

Steve began demanding to see the dailies, which Norman didn't appreciate and this caused anxiety on both sides. In addition, the two men simply had nothing in common, unlike Steve and the director originally attached to the project. Nikita Knatz who worked behind the scenes pointed out, "Remember, McQueen embraced Sam Peckinpah. He was a desert rat like him. Peckinpah drank coffee out of a paper cup. Norman Jewison had his served in a cup and saucer with a spoon. The relationship was hardly father/son. It was more like Mr. Wilson and Dennis the menace."

"In the early scenes we shot, Steve was holding back, not really taking my direction," Norman said in his autobiography. "At the end of one shooting day, we sat down together on the curb of a New Orleans street, the thirty-nine-year-old director, and the thirty-four-year-old star. 'Steve,' I said. 'I don't know what you want from me. Maybe you're looking for a father figure. God knows I can't be that. But I'll tell you what I can be. How about we think of me as your older brother, the one who went to college? I'm the educated older brother and I will always look out for you.' I was just winging it, but this seemed to get his attention. He apparently liked the idea of his director as an older brother"

Norman went on to say, "I'm the guy who's always around taking care of your best interests." Steve appreciated this and they had found their common bond to work from. After that Norman brought their attention to Steve's interest in watching the dailies, "Why do you want to watch them, Steve? You want to check if I'm doing my job? You want to watch yourself? What I think is that the actor should concentrate strictly on his acting. Watching the dailies can throw the actor off. You should forget the dailies. You should rely on your director for guidance. A certain amount of trust is needed on this movie."

Having found their relationship Steve loosened up and never bothered Norman about watching the dailies for the rest of the film. But like a good older brother Norman got the editor to put together a 12-minute sequence of footage shot of Steve to present to him so he could specifically see his "character emerging" as Steve was worried about. "We ran the scenes for him, and afterwards, though he didn't say much, I knew he liked what he saw."

Norman wasn't the only one to feel a little heat from McQueen, actor Karl Malden was thrown into a wall by Steve during one scene. In the film, Steve confronts Karl's character about cheating. "McQueen sprung at me like a tiger. He had the quality of appearing so tense and high that he was ready to explode at any minute." Steve and "potato nose" as he called Karl behind his back worked together again their next film, *Nevada Smith* where Karl learned a little more about why he might have been sprung on so hard. "Our director, Henry Hathaway, invited me to dinner one night specifically to ask me exactly what I had done to Steve McQueen. I told him I hadn't done a thing. Henry informed me that Steve had tried his damnedest to veto my being in the picture. It gnawed at me through the whole shoot; what had I ever done to Steve McQueen? I couldn't imagine until one of the guys at William Morris clued me in. Years before when I had been casting Tea and Sympathy for Kazan in New York, I guess I had seen Steve for the lead, though I had no memory of him. He didn't get the part and, apparently, he held it against me all that time."

"[Edward G.] certainly wasn't a man to be rattled by Steve McQueen on the set. After his first experience with Steve's look-anywhere-but-into-the-eyes-of-my-co-actor form of acting, Eddie said to me, 'Don't worry about anything. I can take care of myself.' And he did." -Norman Jewison

More than a depression era poker movie the film is about the restless up and comer 'The Kid' trying to procure the status of 'The Man'. This pitted Steve McQueen up against Edward G. Robinson as Lancey Howard aka 'The Man'. This was perfect casting as their on screen relations mirrored their private lives. Edward was sitting comfortably in his life as a seasoned actor and a veteran in the motion picture industry whereas Steve was just now coming into his own having fought for every movie and even scene to scene to carve out his place in the industry. "[Steve] was a little nervous about Eddie Robinson, as Eddie was a star," Norman said.

Norman played to Eddie's star ranking when he was trying to persuade him to be in the film. "Look at your entrance in the movie. Lancey arrives in New Orleans by train. He steps onto the platform and a blast of steam comes from under the locomotive. Lancey emerges through the steam like Mephistopheles. The music hits on the sound track, and we get a close-up. He's a figure of mystery. Important. That's how Lancey Howard comes into the movie."

This was Steve's first major film where he is undeniably the lead and with that came a lot that he could lose. "All around that table sat a really solid, first-rate cast, actors who were really sure of themselves—Eddie G, Joan

Blondell, Ann-Margret," which coming from Karl Malden meant something special. "Everyone around that poker table could steal the scene at any moment. We all knew it and that brought a wonderful electricity to the set. Except for the star of the film, Steve McQueen; for him, that knowledge brought only anxiety." But Steve was determined to continue on his path to stardom.

Steve wanted what Eddie had and Eddie didn't want some young punk crowding him. Director Jewison used this to the film's advantage as he kept the two actors apart until the very moment the two men first come into contact on screen. He wanted the actors to hold off sizing each other up until they were on camera. To fuel their competitiveness, Jewison spoke to each actor individually off screen before the cameras ran. He went up to Steve and quietly told him, "You better watch out." Then Jewison casually made his way over to Eddie and said with an air of mistrust, "Watch the kid."

The director's ploy must have struck a nerve with each actor. When the two meet for the first time on screen their words are cordial but the subtext is like two boxers entering a ring for the heavy weight championship. The two men stand facing each other, eyes locked, each waiting for the other to make the first move. Both actors had a habit of completely over taking the films they appeared in because of their ability to captivate audiences. And in this scene their intensity and talent come head to head. "Young star against the old star, look at the way they measure each other," Norman says in the director's commentary about this moment.

Norman Jewison is an actor's director, one who believes in an actors ability to tell a story with their eyes alone. As they begin to play stud poker the film begins to build to a climax in a slow burn as fewer words are spoken in favor of intense close ups revealing the characters inner colors. 'The Kid' is steely-eyed playing the man across from him knowing that with each hand dealt he's that much closer to becoming 'The Man' himself. And 'The Man' sits quietly ever wondering if 'The Kid' really is going to be the one to do him in.

The two characters, as well as the two actors, are toe-to-toe right up to the first break from the game. Everyone is relaxing and Eddie begins to pour himself a drink when Steve walks into frame. Because of their blocking, Steve is upstaged by Eddie so every time he wants to look at Eddie he has to turn his back to the camera, which is a big camera technique no-no and Steve knows that.

This is a precarious position for Steve who counteracts the upstaging in two ways. Jewison always called Steve a "shit-kicking actor" because of his tendency to look down at his feet all the time which made him more interesting to watch. In this scene, Steve looks down often rather than turn his back to the camera and when he does he chooses to only make quick glances to Eddie. In another move Steve conceives of the greatest fly-catching trick of his career, he cuts open a lemon and takes a big bite out of the sour, bright yellow fruit but without puckering his lips. In this simple cunning move, Steve steals the scene as the audience is left thinking about Steve and his sour yellow lemon rather than Edward G. Robinson.

Steve isn't the only one doing the fly-catching however, Eddie is a legendary actor who employs his own thievery and Steve knew that going into filming. One day while Steve and assistant director Kurt Neumann Jr. were getting coffee Steve started talking about how Eddie was going to "destroy him" at some point. Kurt said, "For Steve to predict that was very interesting. It showed how perceptive and instinctive he was. I told Norman what Steve had said and we agreed that we'd just have to watch out for it. And happen it did!"

As 'The Kid' sits stunned at the result of losing the final hand to 'The Man' Steve is in his most vulnerable position of the film. In a stroke of mastery, Edward G. Robinson takes this moment to strike a match. Lighting a match is one of those things that's inherently interesting to watch and Eddie takes full advantage of that. All eyes are transfixed on the match except for Eddie who sells the moment by being so engaged in Steve. Eddie lets the moment sit and doesn't light his cigar allowing the flame to linger, slowly burning down the matchstick dangerously close to burning his fingers as he delivers his final line, "That's life I guess. You're good kid, but as long as I'm around you're second best. You might as well learn to live with it." The fire was out of Steve's eyes during the delivery of this line as he watched Eddie destroy him.

While that was transpiring on film Kurt was watching from behind the camera, "Norman and I were looking at each other, thinking this is getting very tense. The crew was picking up on it also. After that scene, Steve got up and left and we didn't see him for an hour or two. It was one of the cleverest scene-stealing moves of all time and Steve knew it. He had been destroyed by a master."

Eddie Robinson in his autobiography remembers the feeling of delivering his final line to Steve but without the confidence he was able to portray on screen, "I could hardly speak the words. I knew they weren't true. It was I who had to live with it. He was the star, I was second best." And Edie was right. 'The Kid' may have lost the poker game but McQueen came out on top when the film was released. Steve had finally come into his own and this film was to mark the first of five consecutive major movie hits with him as the leading man. And through his authenticity, he was able to bring together everything an actor needs in order to become a bona fide movie star.

"I have nightmares about being poor, of everything I own just vanishing away. Stardom means that can't happen." - Steve McQueen

An article published in 2013 called *The New and Improved Leading Man* featured six distinct factors that contribute to an actor becoming a movie star. What makes *The Cincinnati Kid* special is that this is the first time McQueen has all six factors together in one film.

The first factor is having the right balance of relatability and mystery. Steve looks like the ordinary bar-goer; someone to easily strike up a conversation with and get to know. Even though he was a star he doesn't move the way movie stars seem to move, he doesn't hold himself as someone to be admired or revered on screen or off. Director Franklin Schaffner said, "Success as an actor, and the wealth that has come with it, has never changed the underlying nature of Steve. He's still basically the same youngster whose resistance to any restraints led him to minor encounters with the law." Despite his relatability, there's a reserved side to Steve that makes him mysterious. A brief glance into his eyes tells the story of a complicated inner life.

As 'The Kid,' Steve is able to relax and go on a nice walk with his girlfriend or hang out with his guy friends making him relatable as the everyman. But with something as quick as the turning over of a playing card Steve becomes silent and mysterious. Once he's at the poker table there's no telling what cards he's holding. And Steve never reveals exactly why he won't let his friends help him cheat in the film, he keeps that truth to himself, which hints at a moral code. McQueen is simply someone audiences want to spend time with and try and get to know better.

The second factor that McQueen has in spades is sex appeal. He appeals to both sexes as the type of guy that women want to be with and men want to have a beer with. The first aspect of his on screen sex appeal is his underlining ability to keep his cool under any circumstance, which in his case exudes masculine confidence. But sex appeal doesn't necessarily translate to traditional romanticism. "What I chose to see in Steve from the very start was survival," his second wife Ali MacGraw said. "He was—even when our relationship was deteriorating badly—the person I would most choose to be with in a life-or-death situation. From a romantic point of view, I saw him as the one who would chop down trees to make the fire that would keep away the wild animals, the one who would pull fish out of the stream so that we wouldn't starve to death if we were marooned, the one to find the wild berries for sugar rush. It went way past seeing him as the man who could fix leaky faucets. I knew that in any situation I would never be in fear and danger, as long as I was with him."

There's a multitude of scenes in *The Cincinnati Kid*, which optimizes Steve's sex appeal to both men and women. In one scene The Kid's girlfriend has gone home to her parents and now he's in a compromising position with Melba, the wife of his best friend. She dresses down and comes onto him very strongly, Melba is approaching him and giving off very direct signals about what she wants. 'The Kid' has a sly smile on his face as he already knows what's about to happen and is already enjoying the outcome.

He appears to give her what she desperately wants by accepting a kiss but behind her back, he brings his palm up and slaps her on the ass as if to say "Bad girl." This demolishes Melba's fantasy moment and she grows incredibly angry. She curses him as he coolly walks out of the apartment with the sly grin still imprinted on his face but the moment he's gone Melba wants him even more. In this scene, Steve is both the bad boy to her and the good guy to his friend.

As a leading man and movie star an actor has to have a sense of humor, which is the third factor in being a movie star. Even in action films, an actor can't be the heavy at all times and the ability to laugh at a situation or at oneself aids in making someone more human and real.

Steve as 'The Kid' takes pleasure in being a better gambler than the other characters and here is often where he finds humor. At one of the poker tables a player accuses 'The Kid' of cheating and his response is, "I don't need marked cards to beat you pal." Most other actors would have chosen in this moment to get angry at the accusation and deliver their response with force behind the words but not Steve. Steve's attitude toward the other player conjures up a half smile and he finds humor in the fact that his opponent thinks Steve needs to cheat in order to win.

The fourth factor that contributes is the actor's ability to keep surprising people. Steve as a person and an actor appears to have lived strongly by the motto, "Safety third." All of his major film successes had been gun wielding action roles but he had enough self-knowledge to believe he could carry his identity into other roles. The climax of *The Cincinnati Kid* involves McQueen sitting at a table, not a motorcycle chase or gun fight, he's playing poker and is just as intense as any climax to an action movie.

Throughout his career, Steve would continue to surprise audiences by playing roles that would be expected from other actors. His role of a successful businessman in *The Tomas Crown Affair* would be offered to actors like Rock Hudson and Sean Connery, not the street kid Steve McQueen. And he goes full on Daniel Day-Lewis making himself unrecognizable for his role in one of his last films An *Enemy of the People*, which is based on the classical play by Ibsen and in itself not something audiences expect from McQueen.

The next movie star factor is in the intelligence to recognize your moment. This was the one aspect that hadn't come along for Steve until he did *The Cincinnati Kid*. This is the film where his self-knowledge, maturity, looks, and talent all come together making McQueen feel like a complete package. This is an aspect of becoming a movie star that no one has control over. The best an actor can do is to train hard in preparation so he/she's ready for this moment and even then the piece that connects all of this together is the audience's acceptance.

The sixth and final factor in becoming a movie star is the sense of indispensability. An accumulation of all the factors above Steve is such a sheer force of personality that the audience is engaged when he's on the screen and miss him the moment he walks out of frame. From an industry standpoint, the sense of indispensability is more than loving an actor and wanting to go to every movie they are in but believing that this particular actor is irreplaceable.

There is a sense that if Steve McQueen had never been an actor than the films he stars in would never have been made. McQueen fills the void where Bogart left off and without filling this void the movie industry would feel incomplete. And indeed a niche was empty after he died as action heroes became less human and more robotic or superhuman.

The Sandpebbles
1966

"For me, to do some of these scenes, it's like reaching down into my own stomach and pulling ground glass out."
-Steve McQueen

Neile said she never saw Steve work as hard as he did on *The Sand Pebbles*, a story filled with a rich array of fault filled characters with fears and dreams. Steve's performance, in particular, would be celebrated by moviegoers, critics, and the 1967 film awards circuit. Playing U.S. Naval engineer Jake Holman, Steve received an Oscar nomination for Best Actor in a Leading Role, a Golden Globe nomination for Best Motion Picture Actor, he won a third place Golden Laurel for his dramatic performance, and was named Japan's most popular foreign star for the second consecutive year.

Steve was originally the 7th choice to play Jake Holman, which was six places behind Paul Newman. Getting the movie into production, however, took several years so director Robbert "Bob" Wise went on to make *The Sound of Music*, which won five Oscars including Best Picture and Best Director. Then when he returned to preproduction on *The Sand Pebbles* Steve was a major star and now his first choice to play Holman. If there was ever a perfect part destined for Steve this was the one. Wise said, "He had a great understanding purely for Holman, who was kind of a loner like Steve. Also, Holman loved engines like Steve. And he loved firearms, and Holman had to have a gun, which was right down Steve's Alley." Along with his understanding of the role, Steve filled Jake Holman with his own disposition and temperament to fully bring the role to life. Richard Attenborough said, "His whole being is what you got on screen. You didn't get part of him you got everything."

"You know young actors could sit and watch the way Steve operates logistically as an actor and it's incredible. He makes props a part of what he's doing, which is a wonderful wonderful ability to have in film acting. Steve was always a very physical actor." -Richard Crenna

In the beginning of the film, Holman hauls his bedroll and kit through Shanghai Harbor in route to his new station as an engineer aboard the USS San Pablo. To Steve's credit, he handles his gear as if he's carried this exact kit through dozens of ports just like this one giving a sense of familiarity to Holman's circumstances. So later on when a fellow sailors make comments about Holman having often being transferred from one ship to another the audience has no reason to question the validity of the statements.

Continuing on his way through Shanghai, Holman gets invited to a fancy dinner. During the dinner, Steve takes this opportunity to allude to Holman's past through his behavior and another prop. He looks uncomfortable when he first sits down at the table becoming affixed to the artfully folded napkin on his plate which he doesn't know what to do with, the audience draws the connection that Holman has never had a fancy dinner before. So later on in the film when Holman finally opens up and reveals his troubled past Steve has already planted those seeds so that the information isn't shocking and instead makes him endearing. Earlier in Steve's career, his use of props was almost exclusively about grabbing and holding onto the audience's attention but here those skills have finally evolved into storytelling implements.

When Holman finally gets aboard the American gunboat and closes the access hatch to the engine bay the whole world seems to stand still as this man and machine become aquatinted. "Hello engine, I'm Jake

Holman," he says extending his hand to touch the engine for the first time. Whatever Steve used as an emotional preparation for the first moments of the scene translates to a weary traveler finally coming home to his family. "He was born to play this role," Co-star Richard Crenna says. "Because Steve if you watch him in the film, and we'll see him time and time again his use of what we call in motion pictures props; his use of weapons, his use of the engine. The engine as it is in the story becomes a very important integral part of the story. The engine is a character and Steve plays with that character as if he's playing with another actor. He just brings such a realism to what he does and always did in the film."

The steam engine used in the film was a real working engine reassembled at 20th Century Fox studios. Wise said that Steve learned everything there was to know about operating that ships engine in preparation for the film. This would have been an overwhelming task for most people but Steve had a love of engines. Starting in his teens he was into motorcycles and fast cars. Then when Steve joined the Marines he became a Sherman tank driver with a need for speed. "I'd often wondered if a tank could be speed converted. We figured on haven' the fastest tank in the division. What we got was plenty of skinned knuckles. I found out you can't soup up a tank." Also during his service, Steve was assigned to clean and renovate naval ship engine bays leaving him with a familiarity of the larger ship engines. Afterward, as an acting student in Greenwich Village Steve helped supplement his income as a motorcycle mechanic and even fixed one belonging to James Dean.

By the time Holman gets aboard the USS San Pablo the engine has been neglected and is in need of maintenance and repair. Through his interaction with the engine, Steve is able to elevate and breathe life into the inanimate object as something more than a film prop. Some of the valves he lightly adjusts while other parts of the engine he man-handles all the while monitoring the changes taking place to the rhythm of the machine.

Steve was looking to add credibility to every aspect to his role, which meant doing his homework. In addition to learning lines and doing research, Steve had set out to become proficient with the tools he would need to use on set. Even for something as simple as the ax he uses on screen for less than 30 seconds. In preparation for that scene alone, he carried and practiced with the ax on set for several weeks before filming. The result is an expert like handling and credibility earned.

This same practice was put towards gun handling, which in this film included the Colt 1911 pistol, 1903 Springfield bolt action rifle, and the Model 1918 Browning Automatic Rifle. BAR for short or "Big Ass Rifle" to those who had to carry the 20 pound light machine gun in combat. The BAR was also known to be awkward to operate and slow to reload, however; no one would be the wiser as Steve was able to perform quick reloads and handle the gun in a way that seemed effortless. He kept his strength up during the seven-month shoot in Taiwan by having his gym equipment shipped there, something that seems standard for movie stars today but was unheard of back then.

His use of the 1903 Springfield was also used to great effect the most heartfelt scene of the film. One of Holman's best and only friends has been captured by Chinese Nationals and is being tortured several hundred yards away on the beach. The sailors watch in horror from the San Pablo as their fear of causing an international incident prevents them from taking action. Holman, however; can't take seeing his friend in agony. The script's stage directions for Steve are as follows:

Holman in a sudden rush grabs the rifle away from Restorff and takes aim. Holman, trying to get the aim. Just as Collins starts toward him, Holman fires.

These are simple stage directions and nothing but ink on paper yet Steve brought the actions to life. He acts quickly moving towards his fellow sailor but does more than simply "grabs the rifle away." Steve clutches the rifle with one hand and shoves Restorff away and out of the camera frame with the other. Nothing and no one will stop him now and that determination is visible on his face. He disengages the safety and brings the rifle up to his shoulder. Steve adjusts the elevation in the sights for the proper distance and takes aim. Then he does something unexpected and unscripted, he lifts his head off the rifle with turmoil exuding off of his face looking at his friend and the audience wonders if he'll take the shot. His facial expression changes as he makes the decision, takes aim once again, and fires, recoil punning into his shoulder. McQueen turned these simple stage directions into the film's most heartfelt moment.

Still living truthfully in the scene he becomes aware of the deadly weapon still in his hands and releases the rifle into the river. Po-Han is now dead, Holman being the one who ended his suffering by killing him. Steve in these moments is able to say more with his silence than any other actor could articulate in words. Director Wise said, "I think the sequence where Holman had to shoot Po-Han was my favorite. I thought his whole reaction, when he had to shoot his friend then throw his gun away was just great. Steve did that beautifully. It was clear he wasn't worried about repercussions from his seniors; only thinking of putting his friend out of his misery."

This was not the first time Wise directed Steve in one of his films. Ten years earlier when Steve was a no name actor living in New York City he worked as a $19 a day extra in Wise's film *Somebody Up There Likes Me* starring Paul Newman. McQueen was now a star and held a lot more power in his films, as well he was also head of Solar Productions, which was one of three production companies getting the film made.

Steve was trying to make the best film possible and every Sunday, once they began filming Steve and the crew would get together after a big brunch and watch the dailies. Although called "dailies" the film they shot during the week had to be shipped to LA to be processed then mailed back to Taiwan to be viewed. Watching the dailies became a big event even though the film they watched didn't have any sound.

Steve began getting worried that the film wasn't living up to his vision and he began insisting that all of his scenes be shot the way he envisioned. As a compromise, each scene involving Steve was reportedly shot two different ways, one Steve's way, and one Wise's way. And because of Steve's power on the film, he could have chosen to use only his takes in the final cut; however, according to biographer Marshall Terrill, not a single one of Steve's takes were used as he learned to trust Wise.

Steve knew he had the opportunity to deliver a career-defining performance so one step he made was to make sure none of his fellow actors were going to take any unnecessary attention away from him, as he had done to his leading actors in the past. Behind the scenes he was cautious of his fellow actors and before principal photography began Steve got together with his co-star Richard Crenna. According to Crenna Steve's purpose for this meeting was to figure out if they were going to compete with each other for screen time or collaborate for the betterment of the film. After meeting for ten minutes Crenna said that Steve relaxed once he realized they weren't going to be competing for screen time.

Mako who was the actor playing Po-Han and was also under Steve's watch as he experienced when they were rehearsing a scene together. Mako scratched his head during rehearsal and Steve asked, "Are you going to do that when we shoot for real?" Mako had no idea he was scratching his head so he didn't know what Steve was referring to and when Steve realized this he let the matter go. "In a few days' time, watching him work, I realized what he meant. I had taken one of his tricks away from him." Mako said recognizing that scratching his head at the opportune moment could have stolen the scene away from Steve.

Knowing that his friends wouldn't try to steal any of his thunder Steve lobbied to get two of his good friends aboard as talent. Bud Eakins was a motorcycle riding buddy and the stunt double who performed the famous motorcycle jump in *The Great Escape*. In this film, he played one of the sailors, Restorff, who gets his gun taken away by Holman when he has to shoot Po-Han. Also from *The Great Escape* was Richard Attenborough a British actor who would play the love-struck American named Frenchy. Attenborough is generally regarded as one of the sweetest and kindest actors and who would never purposely take away from another actor.

In the making of a film, hundreds of artists specializing in not only acting and directing but set design, lighting, wardrobe, music, makeup, and more come together to tell a single story. No one field is more important than another even if they would like to think so and because of this emotions run high when paths cross one another. One such situation occurred when Wise was busy setting up a scene and Steve came up to him with an important wardrobe concern that was unrelated to the scene being shot. Wise told him to come back after they had finished shooting for the day. Steve was able to wait for a few hours but the question was burning and he came back to Wise to address the issue. Wise was trying to line up a difficult dolly shot when Steve interrupted, their exchange was quick.

"About those uniforms."
"For Christ's sake! Steve, I told you we'll talk about it later in the day when we finish shooting."

Steve turned and walked away, he was so hurt that his director had turned and blew up on him like that he stopped talking to Wise. "Here I was directing the star of the film and he took directions and he was in the scenes and he would listen to me, but he did not speak one word to me for three days." Eventually, Steve dropped his hard act and started talking to him again once he saw how good the dailies were.

Joe Turkel who was one of the actors playing a sailor on the San Pablo watched Steve every day on set remembering, "Nobody knows this but every day we worked together he was always on time, he was always sober, he always knew his lines and was always ready to work. He didn't take his job as an actor lightly. I worked with Nicholson and he had a reputation as a basketball buff who was a loopy, crazy guy. He was also a fantastic actor. And Steve McQueen, in his own way, had the same reputation, as being a motorcyclist and a drunk who would fool around with a million women and all that. But I tell you, Steve tried his damnedest and worked hard and gave it his all. He was a professional in every sense of the word. He was a conscientious actor. Steve had a tough life and knew he couldn't throw his [career] away." Once Steve and Wise reconciled they didn't have any other issues with each other for the remainder of shooting.

Steve carries with him an exceptionally high level of bravado but on this film, in particular, all the actors seemed to realize that he had reached a new level of his acting. The key lie in his authenticity and as Steve simply put, "Most actors play it up. I'll do it monotone. It's all there. You accept it, or you don't. It comes out of reality." On the first day of training under Sanford Meisner students are taught about "The Reality of Doing," which is to say to do things for real 100%. The concept is a simple one that most actors never master. Doing things for real means there can be no emoting or indicating so when the script says that he should be mad or write something down the actor cannot pretend to be mad or pretend to write something down, the actor must do them for real. Anything less than 100% authenticity Steve considers "Play Acting" and not the business of a true actor.

Wise noted, "I've never worked with a star or any actor who knew what worked for him as well as Steve did. He must have studied himself on screen quite a lot because every so often I would be rehearsing a scene and he would say to me, 'Gee Bob, I think I could get that part over without that line and do it with a reaction', and he was right. He really knew what worked for him."

Also under the "reality of doing" comes the fundamental idea of living truthfully and not through the veil of a character but as one's self. The only character Steve brought to his role as Jake Holman was Steve's own personal character filled with his personal essence as well as his mental and moral qualities. There's a great benefit to using one's own qualities as Richard Attenborough said of Steve, "Because he used his own personality he never did anything false." There is some molding an actor has to do and director Norman Jewison noted that Steve "Tapped into deep parts of himself." In this film, he brought forth his loner qualities and his mistrust of authority in order to find the role within himself rather than create an entirely new external character. Character as far as any script is concerned is the sum of actions performed within a role and Steve made those actions to be as authentic as possible adding credibility to his role and to the film.

Critics raved about Steve, Bosley Crowther of the *New York Times* said his performance is "the most restrained, honest, heartfelt acting he has ever done." In this film, Steve breathes life into the role by bringing his personal character to Holman and he goes the extra mile in making all of his actions real. Everything he does is biased on truth and he doesn't pretend to do anything. The result of this combination is an Academy Award nomination for Best Actor in a Leading Role.

Candice Bergen who played Steve's love interest in the film said, "[He] brought a tremendous amount of conflict and it was a very powerful performance. It was complicated, very loaded emotionally, very charged performance. It was almost like he was in a coiled position and very torn, very emotionally torn you really felt the sorta emotional charge that Steve brought to it that really coincided with [Holman]."

Films In Review also picked up on the internal struggle to which he brought to Holman, "McQueen has a cerebral vitality which is absorbing to watch. No matter what the situation, he seems always to be possessed of more moral force than he's using." And *The Hollywood Reporter* noted how the internal struggle manifested in his acting, "McQueen is a unique actor, one of remarkable conviction, and one who can project subtleties of character and development with a flick of his eyes or a slight shift of body [language]."

Consistency is the key to McQueen's Oscar-nominated performance, every moment of every scene is great acting where every moment tells a story right down to and including a slight pat Steve gives the engine. Not only does *The Sand Pebbles* mark Steve's first critically acclaimed performance but this film marks an evolution in his acting. Before this film Steve's use of props and physicality were specifically used to gravitate the attention of the audience towards himself, now those skills were solely used to bring authenticity to the role and to tell a complete story.

The Sand Pebbles was nominated for 8 Oscars and Steve went on his first big run of promoting a film, which involved multiple interviews and appearances on TV's most popular live programs including *What's My Line?*, *The Ed Sullivan Show*, and *The Tonight Show* with Johnny Carson. Then he became the 153rd star to leave his handprints and signature at Grauman's Chinese Theater in Hollywood. In classic McQueen fashion, he became the first star to sign the cement in the reverse direction of everyone else's signature. Not one to turn his back on a camera this was done so that the crowd of two thousand could watch him more easily.

The other actors nominated for Best Actor in a Leading Role included Alan Arkin, Michael Caine, Richard Burton, and Paul Scofield who ended up winning for his performance in *A Man for All Seasons*. Neile wasn't too upset that her husband had lost, "If he'd won, he'd have been impossible to live with. Not because of a big head but because he'd be worrying how to top himself next." At a party, after the Academy Awards, Steve turned to Mako, who had been nominated for Best Actor in a Supporting Role as Po-Han, and said, "Ah fuck 'em all, next time we get 'em."

The Thomas Crown Affair
1968

"I believe in lots of preparation. I want to look the part of the character I'm playing. It takes time. It takes study. It takes a deep understanding of the character involved." - Steve McQueen

Alan Trustman was a lawyer and attorney who had never written before writing *The Crown Caper*. A story about a sophisticated bank heist in Boston masterminded by a rich gentleman named Thomas Crown. In the story, everything goes according to Crown's plan until afterward when he pushes his luck with a crafty female insurance investigator. Director Norman Jewison got ahold of the story and loved the idea of directing what he called, "a love story between two shits."

Jewison and Trustman got together and worked on flushing out the script for the next 15 months renamed The Thomas Crown Affair. He wanted a film that was more "style over content" and the two of them were thinking of actors such like Cary Grant and Sean Connery for the leading role as they were looking for the feel of an American James Bond.

Jewison and executive producer Walther Mirisch first began courting Sean Connery for the role. "They went after Connery for many months," Trustman says. "But it all ended one crazy week in New York where Norman Jewison and Walther Mirisch stayed at the Sherry Netherland Hotel and Connery was nearby at The Plaza. They all met for an hour every day but Connery couldn't make up his mind so they went back to Los Angeles."

"I thought of changing my image for more than a year. I felt it was time to get past those tough, uptight types." - Steve McQueen

Steve and his wife were eating breakfast when she turned to him and said, "Gee honey that's too bad, you know, Norman doesn't want you for *The Crown Caper* because I think you could do it." Steve stopped eating his french toast and replied, "What are you talking about?" Always good at picking out scripts that would be perfect for Steve, Neile was covertly trying to get him to want to play the lead role. She said, "Well you know Norman wants either Sean Connery or Rock Hudson for this part, it's unfortunate you know because you could be, I think, really terrific in it." "You got to be kidding me what do you mean he doesn't want me?" And when she told him that the script had been given to everyone in Hollywood except him, Steve was then adamant that no one but him play the title character.

Steve and Norman had worked together on *The Cincinnati Kid* and Steve began calling him regularly about the part. Norman Jewison's first reaction to the thought of Steve in the role was "Over my dead body will that guy play Thomas Crown. How can Steve McQueen possibly imagine himself in this movie."

No one wanted Steve for the part except for Steve and his wife. "I was advised not to do it." Steve said, "They told me it would be like trying to make a silk purse out of a sow's ear. But I said wait a minute, this dude wants to show he can beat the establishment at its own game. He's essentially a rebel, like me. Sure, a high-society rebel, but he's my kind of cat. It was just his outer fur that was different - so I got me some fur."

A little more than their clothing was different, Steve only had a 9th-grade education, which he got from The Boys Republic and Thomas Crown was a Phi Beta Kappa from Dartmouth. "He lives a cultured and high styled life, he has a butler and a Boston townhouse and he has lots of money. This is not Steve McQueen you know?" Jewison says, "Steve McQueen grew up in boys town without a father and never had anything in his life and was streety and not very well educated. I don't think Steve had much interest in reading books but he knew one thing, he wanted desperately to play this character. And so because he wanted to play the part and I wasn't too sure if he should there was that relationship that I could have with him in the film where he really became very dependent on me to play this kind of character, this kind of sophisticated cynical romantic protester from the upper class. And he really had to talk me into letting him play the part."

When Jewison realized that he wasn't going to get Sean Connery and went back to LA Steve made a visit to his house in Brentwood. Steve's intention was to convince Jewison that he was Thomas Crown and he succeeded. Norman came around to the idea because they had worked well together in the past and he knew that Steve would rely on his directing ability to pull off the role. Not to mention he realized that with Steve the film would make a lot of money.

"When I heard McQueen was cast, I was furious as I thought there was no way he could play an upper-class aristocrat," said writer Alan Trustman. "But they told me to get used to the idea." Embracing the situation Trustman went to United Artists and got ahold of every film and television show Steve had ever done. "I then went down to New York and spent 16 hours a day in a hotel room screening McQueen and making notes on what he could do and what he couldn't do, what made him comfortable, what made him uncomfortable."

Trustman recognized common themes in Steve's acting and figured out that when possible Steve would fall back on certain characterizations to which he knew audiences liked seeing him in. "By the end of that week, I felt I really knew McQueen and I rewrote the script for him."

During this process, Trustman also realized Steve could be the next Humphrey Bogart and explained that to him

"You are shy; you don't talk too much. You are a loner but a person with integrity. You're quiet; you're gutsy as hell. You like girls but are basically shy with women. You have a tight smile, and you don't show your teeth, but it's a small smile around your mouth and you never deliver a sentence more than five or ten words long because paragraphs make you lose interest or something goes wrong with your delivery. As long as you can stay with that, you can be No.1."

As for activities, Jewison explained to Trustman that Steve always had to be given something physical to involve himself in, being machinery or horses and that's where the dune buggy and polo scenes came into being.

Steve loved the new version of the script and said of Trustman, "I don't know how, but the son of a bitch knows me." With a script tailored to McQueen, he didn't need to try and change his essence to what someone would intellectually think Thomas Crown to be. Steve already had the presence to pull off the role in a straightforward manner. He has an adventurous feel and is the type of guy who is always looking for new thrills, which is what leads Crown from playing polo, driving dune buggies on the beach, flying gliders, and pulling off bank heists.

McQueen began preparing for a role unlike any other he had played before but he did so in staying true to his system of familiarity and practice of action. Actions are what makes Steve authentic in his film roles. Steve learned to play chess and how to drink out of a brandy snifter. He practiced polo for three weeks until his hands bled so that he could even give the professionals a run for their money.

Not surprisingly Steve needed that same amount of time (and a six-figure sum for his clothing budget) to master wearing a suit as his co-star Faye Dunaway mentioned in her autobiography *Looking for Gatsby*.

Steve even tried his hand at doing a Boston accent, which Jewison didn't like so at his advice Steve tried a more "clipped" accent and to annunciate more to make him sound more educated. Also, Steve and his friends are the ones who built the dune buggy so there was no learning curve once he was strapped in and driving on set.

There was, however, one liberty Steve took concerning the memorization of his lines, more specifically he didn't bother to memorize them. Steve would read the script over and over again but had grown accustomed to waiting to memorize his lines until he was on set. In the past, this had given him the chance to explore his actions fully before locking himself into the dialogue, plus he always liked cutting out his dialogue anyway for a less is best approach.

This laze-fair attitude to the memorization of his lines backfired as Neile remembers in her memoirs, "On the first day of rehearsing *Thomas Crown* Steve arrived on the set totally unprepared for Faye Dunaway's brand of professionalism. She already had her character and her dialogue nailed down. He came home that evening awed by Faye, who had come to work 'so ready, so prepared that she threw everything at me but the kitchen sink! I couldn't believe it!' As soon as dinner was over he and I spent the next few hours on the script memorizing his lines. Norman Jewison was not going to see him again lagging behind his less experienced co-star."

Previous to this incident occurring Steve was upset Faye was cast because she was a relatively new actress to big films and her hit film *Bonnie and Clyde* had not yet to been released, for which she earned her first Academy Award nomination. Steve was calling her "Dun-fade-away" behind her back but after this first day of rehearsals and as their professional relationship grew he began referring to her as "The Great Lady." The feeling was returned as she said she saw him as an icon and the two built a mutual respect for one another. "We had both grown up on the wrong side of the tracks," Faye said. "But by the time I got to *Thomas Crown*, I'd shaken off anything that might hint of that. Steve, on the other hand, never stopped feeling he was a delinquent and any day he'd be found out."

In his time spent studying the Meisner technique Steve was trained how to build a relationship. And like everything else he did he worked to make that action as real and authentic as possible. "Steve had so much charisma and he seemed to trigger those nurturing instincts in women. He was a chauvinist - legendary in that he was - but a chivalrous one to me. There was a strange dynamic between us," said Faye.

The most famous scene between Steve and Faye is the chess scene in which every moment hides a sexual innuendo. This scene is filled with close up and extreme close up shots of the actors faces. With the magic of film editing, Steve and Faye appear to be looking directly into each other's eyes but this wasn't the case on set. Jewison reviled that because the cameras were so big and had to be so close to the actors faces that they could only film one actor at a time and each actor was actually looking at pieces of tape stuck to the camera for their eye lines.

For Steve, Jewison would describe what Faye would be doing if she was acting in front of him in order to elicit the desired response and vice versa for Faye. They were able to pull this off because even though Steve and Faye were not rooted in a connection with one another they lived truthfully under the given imaginary circumstances.

Modern actors are often concerned with being present with their scene partners and in having organic moments but this can't always be the case because of the restraints of filmmaking. In this scene, Steve and Faye are able to take direction and create their own moments individually.

Many actors have difficulty in taking direction because they try to figure out, intellectually, how the direction makes sense within the context of the scene rather than using the scene as a basis for the direction.

Nikita Knatz who was a sketch artist for the production said, "Jewison had McQueen doing what he wanted to do all along. The chess game—it looks like McQueen ad-libbed it. It was all predesigned by Jewison." Steve trusted Jewison's vision and fully placed himself into the hands of his director.

Another example is when Crown has pulled off the heist and is relaxing in his home. The part in the scene where Crown begins laughing and dancing around the room was improvised on set by Jewison and although McQueen was hesitant and embarrassed at the thought he did as he was directed. The result is one of the first times we see Steve let loose on film.

"If you put Steve on an empty stage with a chair and a soliloquy to read, he wouldn't hold an audience. That took acting [like that of] Laurence Olivier. But if I asked Steve to walk across a room for the camera, he would be natural and immensely appealing. Olivier would act the walk of a character. Steve would simply walk. The audience would be more convinced by Steve than Olivier." -Norman Jewison

Emotionally, Steve's performances on *The Thomas Crown Affair* is on par with many of his other films in that he rarely puts his emotions out on display. Many actors today are the opposite, often they reach for as many emotions as they can regardless of what is called for in the script simply to prove they are "good" actors. Actors in this same category commonly use devices like putting mentholated rub under the lash line of each eye to make their eyes swell up and tear in order to simulate them feeling an emotion. Showing emotions simply for emotion's sake does not make a good actor and these fake crocodile tears will never form a connection with audiences.

Steve's approach to emotions was biased in the fact that in day to day life most people try to hide their real emotions. Imitating this human quirk is often a trap that many lesser actors fall into. Reaching emotions is a strenuous and unpleasant task so many actors use this human quirk as an excuse to not feel anything. They say they're hiding their true emotions when in reality they aren't feeling a damn thing, which makes them appear dead inside.

The truthful way to do this as Steve does is to become emotionally full and then try to hide the emotion. "Steve dislikes open emotions." Neile said, "He believes that the true nature of man is how much he can feel without showing it." But even though he's not overtly showing his emotions they are still influencing his behavior and that allows audiences to connect with him.

A byproduct of this inward aspect to McQueen's character is, strangely enough, a sense of vulnerability. Although this is a quality that is often associated with weakness this is not the case with Steve. His vulnerability lies only in the context of his masculine strength of not overtly showing his emotions. Jewison believes that this vulnerability is partly to credit as to what makes Steve so fascinating as a film star and proves that actions speak louder than words and behavior speaks louder than action.

Steve McQueen is a very clever actor and turns an otherwise ordinary dramatic role into something much cooler. Most leading men/women act throughout a dramatic story as if they're losing the fight of their lives and the audience follows along in their struggle to the ultimate victory, the harder the struggle means the greater the triumph. McQueen on the other hand plays Thomas Crown as someone who's always on top of things. He throws an acting curve ball by acting as if he's already achieved ultimate victory and triumph and the audience is engaged, not out of compassion but because people love winners.

When *The Thomas Crown Affair* premiered and was a gigantic success the world responded with a loud "We didn't know McQueen had that in him." Steve shook up the public's expectation of him by reshaping himself without becoming unrecognizable. With the right amount of self-awareness and arrogance, he was able to play against type and surprise everyone.

'Bullitt'
1968

"I don't know a young actor, who wanted to be a star, who hasn't studied *Bullitt* again and again and again... This is a complete performance where every single bit of physical action has its unique power. " -Lawrence Kasdan

McQueen was moving up in the industry in a big way. In the late 60's Steve's production company, Solar, signed a 6 picture deal with Warner Brothers and moved their production headquarters onto the Warner lot.

Solar's executive producer Robert Relyea said, "We had been at Warner's for about three months and when a studio makes these deals, they expect productivity. So one night Steve and I were chatting at one of our offices and we knew we had to move on something, whatever it was, and Steve said, 'I think we better do the cop thing." That "cop thing" Steve was talking about would become McQueen's most iconic role.

When Neile first brought up the idea of her husband playing the title role of *Bullitt* Steve shot down the idea, "No way I'm playin' a cop, those kids call 'em pigs, man. What are you trying to do to me? Why those kids would turn on me so fast it'd make your head spin!" Not until Steve looked past himself at the world around him did he change his mind, "We're in the midst of anti-war demonstrations, anti-authority movements, and the drug culture and I think I can do something different'." Steve believed he could do some good by changing the public's perception of cops so he began putting a team in place to help him do just that.

Bullitt started off as Robert L. Pike's book *Mute Witness*. Alan Trustman was brought on to do the adaptation of the book, which was not a simple process,

"[Pike's] book was about a 67-year-old Jewish detective in New York City. There was no character of Bullitt, no girl, there was no Mustang, no car chase, no airport chase, no hospital chase. When I read Pike's book I told Flaxman, 'This is ridiculous, I can't adapt this, there's nothing here'. And he said, 'Well write an original and we will say it's an adaptation.' So I wrote *Bullitt*, in one day."

This was not the typical film script as Robert Vaughn found out, he was offered the role of Walter Chalmers the control hungry politician but twice he turned the part down as he found the script too confusing.

"Do you know what a hook is?" Trustman asked, "A hook is a device you use to keep the audience in their seat. If you go out to buy the popcorn during the picture, you're going to miss one line and you won't understand the movie and the confusion is deliberate. There is an inherent plot, and you don't pull it off on the screen. It's the opposite of television. A television audience gets infuriated if they don't understand what's going on every five minutes. A movie audience is locked into it by the confusion." Eventually, Vaughn's confusion went away when he was offered more money and he accepted the role.

Trustman was not the only writer on the project, Harry Kleiner was brought on to help incorporate McQueen's own ideas into the script. Even though Trustman left the project after a few too many changes were made the confusion aspect to the script was kept in to allow the audience to do their own detective work.

When the time came to choose a director Solar put together a list of 100 possibles then narrowed that down to 5. They called their first choice but the line was busy, they didn't waste any time and immediately called their second choice but there was no answer. Steve had a good feeling that their third pick would be home as he was living in England where the time was 3:00am and he was likely asleep. "Good he'll be home," Steve said as he dialed Peter Yates who answered the call and would take on the role of director.

"Peter had tremendous enthusiasm and he had a real good slant on *Bullitt* from the beginning," cinematographer William Fraker said. "Peter was honest and there was never any bullshit about him, like Steve in a way."

When the rest of the team was put together they went back to Warner to get their permission and a go-ahead on the film. But Jack Warner didn't understand something, "Why does Steve want to do a movie about a cop when we're having anti-war demonstrations and anti-authority is an all-time high in this country?" Robert Relyea told him Steve's intentions with the role and Jack understood, giving the team almost complete control over the making of the film.

Bullitt is the film where Steve would announce to the world he was a filmmaker and wanted the respect of the industry. Steve was looking at the world around him and wanted to take part in the upheaval that he saw was taking place in the industry. "I think that more so than any other time in the history of motion pictures, people in college are taking their Super 8-mm cameras and going out and shooting film. Before long, in the near future, they'll probably bypass the motion picture industry as far as technique is concerned because there is freedom and improvisational freedom at that."

Steve and Yates had a lot of ideas on what the film should be and represent. "We're trying to show what a cop could be like, Steve said. "Everybody dislikes cops till they need one." They wanted to show the police as real human beings. But the police weren't the only ones they were leaving a progressive comment on, in one scene on an operating table a white nurse wipes the brow of a black doctor. These were the years of the civil rights movement and Steve, who was against racism, thought that moment was important to keep in the movie.

Peter Yates was on board and looking to bring something new to American cinema. Yates said, "There had been too many police pictures made, too many television pictures made that we just had to keep away from the normal, what is expected."

This was also the first major film to use the word "Bullshit" and the first time Steve allowed a swear word to be in one of his films. The moment comes at one of Frank Bullitt's most emotional points in the film, Solar had to fight to keep this in as the line is more about the emotion than the word itself.

Steve's good buddy Loren James had more to say on what Steve decided to put in his movies, "If he got a script and they told him they wanted to put in a nude scene of either him or the girl or a lot of swearing he'd say, 'Not a Steve McQueen movie. If my acting isn't good enough to where we have to put that stuff in there to make it worth while. No thank you.'"

"It was [McQueen's] first picture as a producer, his first picture with his own company and he was determined that he was going to set up a way of working that gave a lot of sympathy to directors and to actors." -Peter Yates

Steve and Peter wanted to make the film as realistic as possible and every possible step was taken to bring about reality in the film. This starts with shooting entirely on location. "Sure we could shoot in the studio but I think we're getting into an era where pictures are more visual," Steve said. "The audiences are more sophisticated. They're not accepting substitutes."

The films shooting location was moved to San Francisco and away from Hollywood to gain more freedom. This came with the added bonus with the mayor of San Francisco giving them a free run over the city and allowing them to use the police station, international airport, the general hospital as well as many other locations.

In addition, as many actors as possible were replaced with real people; real police officers, ambulance drivers, architects, nurses, and doctors were all used for scenes in which they were performing their daily duties. In one hospital scene a real doctor almost cut into the actor on the table with a scalpel as the moment was so real to him. "The feelings, the sensitivities that was in that hospital this is the kind of reality that's important in motion pictures," Steve said. "If you try to act it it doesn't really come across as if you're really doing it."

Steve and Peter were trying to make their film look more like a documentary than a studio film with a story that's more true to life than the cookie cutter Hollywood movies. In order to help achieve this, they shot in low light levels with specifically designed lenses and faster film stock. Steve explained, "I think the film should be of a more impressionistic nature, that you shouldn't have to dot all the I's and cross all the T's. We want a feeling of realism that the audience can participate in the action."

The hotel that was shot in was especially true to life. In real life, the hotel was The Hotel Kennedy, which during that time was described by local Tony Plazza as "lodgings for alcoholics, drug users, and the near destitute—with a few prostitutes thrown in for good measure." Robert Relyea said, "That hotel really was a hotel, it was not a set and the elevator really was an elevator in that cheesy hotel. In fact, when we brought in two police experts to help us with the bullet holes and the body marking after the killing, one guy said, 'You know, I did one of these a couple of months ago in this same room, but it wasn't for a movie."

When the time came to shoot the scene of McQueen walking in to view the hotel crime scene after the murder his reactions were improvised. Peter Yates hid a few items in the room and had told Steve to try and find them, which produced the natural reactions in Steve's face and added more realism to the film.

Steve was only trying to do for the film what he strove for in his acting, which was to be as real as possible. Whether he was in a military uniform, cowboy hat, three piece suit, or carrying a badge Steve McQueen held onto his essence. He had made contact with his essential self and was confident enough to put that out on display for the world to see on screen. Actress Nancy Malone said, "He was a tough guy, and everything he portrayed was the real Steve McQueen. When you saw him, it wasn't as if you were watching Laurence Olivier with a fake nose or a hunch back. There was always a bit of Steve in his parts."

Employing his natural essence could be why Steve always regarded himself as a "reactor" rather than an actor. He would tell his directors, "I'm a reactor, don't give me too much dialogue." Peter Yates disagrees and believes Steve "dealt very well with dialogue" but he would also attest to Steve's ability to react truthfully under the given imaginary circumstances. Yates said about the ambulance ride scene with his wounded partner, "You could always rely on McQueen to show his real feelings with his eyes. I mean they're extraordinary, you can see how upset he is and really worried he is by the fact that the person he is responsible for, his junior. His eyes here you can tell he was genuinely worried and felt responsible and this is what sets off his whole chase."

There are other reasons for Steve wanting less dialogue in the film rather than to just play to his strengths and that has to do with camera time. In order to give meaning to what's being said the camera is often directed at the person doing the listening rather than the talking. Watching someone's reactions to what's being said tells the audience what direction the film is headed. Steve even told the writer of the script Harry Kleiner, "I don't want to talk, give the speeches to the guys in the pressed suits, I'd rather react." This also gives the exposition to the other actors so when Steve does speak he has more meaningful and revealing things to say. McQueen was a very intelligent actor and realized, "You only say what's important and you own the scene."

"I have a good feeling about how to make a cop very interesting." -Steve McQueen

"Over the years Steve had developed his own way of preparing for a role," Neile said. "He discussed and dissected his character with his directors and co-stars for hours, and researched the role as well, mostly by observing people." This film was no different, even though Steve wanted to do something innovating with Frank Bullitt, he knew he had to start with something real.

In doing homework for the role Steve did ride-alongs with the San Francisco Police Department and shadowed Detectives John McKenna and Dave Toshi. Steve gained a lot of insight during this time, "I wanted to see the inside. I saw more than I counted on. I got my head twisted. I was raised in the streets and never liked cops much. But here I am right in the middle of real police business. Man, it's different from the inside. I see 75 suspects paraded in the lineup; over half of them armed... I'm playing a real cop and I can imagine going up against that... Seven homicides in one week while we're shooting around the investigations to get the story of a fictional homicide. Real and fiction get mixed in a very strange way."

During the process of preparing for the role Steve was present with police for riots, drug busts, and he also visited crime victims in hospitals. Anything to help him get a better understanding of what the detectives experience emotionally. And their lack of emotion at seeing the dead bodies in the city morgue could be what prompted Steve to develop a plan for their next visit. Steve called Yates one day to invite him down to the morgue and telling him,

"The police took me in there and it's very effective. This time I'm gonna go - I'm going to eat an apple in there because I want to show them that it doesn't affect me at all."

One event that did have an emotional impact was when John McKenna and Dave Toshi finally apprehended a real killer they were after. They were obsessed with bringing him in and when they finally did, the killer hung himself in his cell. After this Robert Relyea noted, "The officers went into a strange state of mind. I think Steve got very bothered. He felt he got a hook on what they were like. He knew them well enough to know what they were going through. The months of paperwork, computer work, and then they caught the guy and he still cheated them. I think that Steve got a real fix on what police work was like. He really understood those two detectives."

Steve was able to bring his emotional understanding of what a homicide detective goes through and breathe life into his role of Frank Bullitt. Although not everyone is personally familiar with the life of a homicide detective, the emotions are universal and that's the aspect that makes Frank Bullitt both identifiable and relatable to the audience. After that point, the camera finds him irresistible because he is not alone on the screen but connected with the audience.

Helping Steve and the other actors get to the point of being identifiable and relatable is the rehearsal process. As a producer, Steve was able to schedule two weeks of rehearsal before principle photography began, which was unheard of during this time. Director Peter Yates noted, "He felt it gave the actors more control, which of course it does because they've had a chance of trying out exactly what they wanted to do and my chance of telling them exactly how I saw the characters and how I saw the part." Steve equally enjoyed the rehearsals and when that process ended he "got up and made a really lovely speech," according to Peter. Steve said, "You know, this shows people that the actors are important in Hollywood and that this is a turn of events."

With his essential self and an emotional understanding of the role, Steve was able to be believable as Lt. Frank Bullitt. A no nonsense anti-authoritarian cop who will stop at nothing in order to do what he feels is right.

The first scene in the film humanizes Frank, he's in bed being woken up by his detective partner Delgetti. As Steve gets out of bed to let Delgetti in through the front door his legs are stiff going down the stairs and he is yawning trying to wake up his body. His eyes are only half open and haven't yet adjusted to the morning light. Once inside Delgetti pours a glass of orange juice and walks towards Frank who begins to stretch out his weary hand thinking the glass is for him but Delgetti walks past drinking the orange juice himself. Steve is momentarily saddened and he begins to get a little cranky for having his sleep interrupted and now his juice stolen by his unapologetic partner. This moment doesn't propel the story but instead allows audiences a glimpse into Franks life making him more relatable.

Once he is awake and on the job he is entirely focused on the task at hand. Most leading actors in dramatic role play as if they are constantly losing to overwhelming odds and constantly fighting harder to over come obstacles. Steve does something different but equally dramatic and engaging. He believes in himself, knows he's going to win, and has absolute confidence in his abilities that he will get the job done. He also brings this same attitude when his superiors try to get him to play their game, he restrains himself then does what he feels is right often ignoring them completely. Bullitt refuses to give in or even fight with his superiors because he knows, in the end, they will thank him for making the right calls.

In a hospital scene when the action has slowed down, Bullitt is eating a sandwich when Chalmers enters the small room. This is a scene between Steve McQueen and Robert Vaughn. Bullitt watches as Chalmers closes a window giving the two men privacy. Bullitt knows his head is on the chopping block because the witness he was supposed to be protecting has been shot and is in critical condition. Chalmers begins his investigation of Bullitt who in return begins his investigation of Chalmers. Steve chooses to play the scene cool and collected as if he's several steps ahead of Chalmers while he continues to eat his sandwich and drink his milk. Not until Bullitt brings up his fellow officer who's been shot does he change his tone but he still keeps his emotions in check, not allowing them to overcome his judgment. Bullitt begins to go on the offensive and Chalmers only defense is to threaten him. Bullitt smiles, he doesn't believe Chalmers can hurt him, he knows he's right and allows Chalmers to have the last word and walk out.

The scene is a very pleasurable one to watch, by choosing the high ground McQueen plays the epitome of cool. He reacts in this scene the way most people only dream about talking to their bosses and he does this effortlessly. "Movie stars are essentially canvases upon which people project their own feelings, desires, and needs", Ben Affleck says. "His canvas was broad and many people could relate to it."

McQueen was careful not to appear to superhuman though and in the middle of the film Steve puts his detective work aside and the 'King of Cool' goes grocery shopping. He parallel parks his muscle car on a quiet street and walks to the small shop at the corner of Clay and Taylor stopping just outside to get a news paper. He checks his pockets for change and when he realizes he doesn't have any he shows no self-pity. Steve reacts as if this is a common occurrence and quickly commits petty theft popping open the coin operated newspaper rack and taking one. Peter said, "That again was an idea of Steve's, he felt that it showed humanity." Steve didn't even check to make sure the coast is clear until after the crime is committed.

With his newspaper in hand, Steve walks in the store seemingly grabbing food at random. "I think I should take one of everything," Steve said. "I'm not interested in food as a character and I think that I should just show that food is really quite unimportant to me." With a paper bag full of random vegetables and assorted TV dinners he pays and walks out as peacefully as he walked in. Talking about the scene Yates said, "That's a quiet no dialogue moment that really says so much about his character."

One of the aspects that the Meisner technique focuses on is making a commitment and devoting oneself to completing independent activities. Throughout all of his films but is especially evident in this one is Steve's way of making monotonous actions exciting. Independent activities as simple as getting dressed into a blue turtle neck and shoulder holster are charged with his own breed of masculine energy. Peter noted, "McQueen's movement is extraordinary, it's so relaxed and it is a complete study in movement. He never makes a bad move and his little gestures and things are what gave him his character I think. The way he moved like a panther."

In another scene, Bullitt and Delgetti go through two luggage trunks looking for clues. In preparation for the scene, McQueen and Don Gordon had watched real detectives go through this procedure so they would know how to do the task properly when the time came to film. Peter packed the prop trunks so that Steve and Don wouldn't know exactly what's in them or where the items they were told to look for are hidden. They were told to look out for items like plane tickets, money, and passports as clues. The scene that unfolded was completely improvised, with the insert shots added afterward.

A directing strategy like this eliminates the actor's intellect when playing the scene. Peter said that they loved playing this scene and felt they were really discovering the items themselves as actors. Steve and Don were simply responding to the items they naturally found in the trunks. If they would have known exactly where every item was and when they were supposed to find them that anticipation would have taken them out of the moment making they're acting less truthful.

"We chose Jacqueline Bisset for the film because I felt that she had very sincere quality to her, when you're choosing a girl to play opposite Steve McQueen you have to be very very careful because he doesn't look the kind of man who would have a girl who was in any way painted or presented with a feeling of insincerity." -Peter Yates

Throughout the film, there are moments that break up the drama and police procedures to show another side of Bullitt. Franks girlfriend Cathy played by Jacqueline Bisset is often at the center of these scenes. Peter said, "We were using her as a comment on McQueen, showing McQueen's sympathetic side."

The first time they are together in the film is unique in that the scene displays their affection for one another but only after revealing their differences. They are from two different worlds, she is cultured and European with a college education and a job as an architect whereas Bullitt is a product of the streets. Yet they're a beautiful couple together and their relationship is absolutely believable bringing more depth and humanity to the film.

The Coffee Cantata scene shows an earnest depiction of how they interact with one another. The scene that's in the film was improvised after the initial scripted scene didn't produce what they wanted. Yates decided to take the camera outside and let the actors react naturally to having dinner together. They were able to relax and the moments that follow are honest and real.

Looking through the window and into their dinner provides a glimpse into Bullitt's romantic private life. Although their dialogue can't be heard their interaction with one another speaks volumes. They're enjoying their time together and one look in particular from Steve says all that's needed to set up the next scene. He looks at her like a man who knows he's getting laid that night.

Cut to Frank and Cathy in bed together, her hair is tousled and she appears to be sleeping when the phone rings. He tries not to wake her and talks quietly but when he hangs up Cathy's awake and asks about the call. Bullitt gives her the cold shoulder and won't tell her, only that she needs to go back to sleep. This is an odd moment for a couple that seemed perfect for one another but the moment plants the seeds for the relationship conflicts to follow.

Over the course of filming Jacqueline Bisset's role in the film got progressively smaller. "I suppose I was the aesthetic part of his life," Jacqueline said of her place with Steve, which isn't too far off from Cathy's relationship with Frank in the film. Cathy wants to be more apart of Franks life but he won't open up emotionally. Bullitt has to be tough in his line of work and distance himself emotionally in order to do a good job but he has problems turning that off when he's with Cathy. He has a difficulty sharing and is often distant. Frank is a flawed character but this also makes him human and all the more gratifying when he finally does emotionally let his guard down for her.

"[Mcqueen] was doing the best he could and he was never shy about asking the same of his coworkers. He would ask, 'Are we all doing the best we can?" -Robert Relyea

Everyone involved in pre-production seems to have a quote taking credit for putting the car chase in the movie but all that matters is the 9 minutes and 42 seconds of cinematic gold that ended up on screen. The chase was the birth of an icon and the embodiment of Steve.

Highland green Mustang Fastbacks are now synonymous with Steve McQueen but in the beginning, when the concept of having a car chase scene in the film, the script simply said, "CHASE." Obviously, they did some elaboration once they got on set. Peter said, "Steve and I were great admirers of drivers and of driving. And we were determined to show the skill of driving as opposed to the pure demolition derby."

Like everything Steve does the driving had to be real and pointing out the shots of him driving are easy. Always keenly aware of the camera's relation to him he would adjust the Mustang's rearview mirror so that his face would be visible in the interior shots. Then for the exterior shots, he kept his face as close to the open window as possible so there wouldn't be any question who was doing the driving.

Warner Brothers Studio had a deal with Ford that they would use Ford's in all their films which are why the new 1968 Mustang 390 GT was chosen but Steve and Peter didn't want a Ford chasing a Ford so through Steve's power they were given permission to use the 1968 Dodge Charger 440 Magnum as the second car. This same principle was applied to choosing two different airline companies so no one would get the impression they were advertising.

Like the rest of the film, they made the chase as real as possible by filming at high speeds topping over a hundred miles an hour. There are no quick cuts, in-distinguishable actions, or excessive shaky-cam's that are so prevalent in modern action scenes. This allows the audience to bear witness to the reality of the danger. They also made the decision not to overlay the action with music, instead of letting the raw power of the two muscle cars dominate the audio.

In the end when the bad guys have been beaten and Bullitt's good name restored he goes home to his girlfriend. Frank opens the door to his bedroom and sees Cathy lying in bed asleep. After checking on her he turns around and puts his gun and holster down before entering the bathroom. Watching someone decide not to do something is inherently interesting and here Bullitt turns on the water and acts like he's about to wash his face in the sink but instead he stops. He raises his head up to the mirror and peers into his eyes as if reading his autobiography. He looks as though he's sad about something possibly even regretful. Maybe his girlfriend was wrong when she thought these things don't affect him. Whatever the cause of the emotion Steve clearly shows the audience that this is not the end of the story and that life will continue on for Lt. Frank Bullitt.

Steve McQueen succeeded in doing something that had never been done with a cop before on screen, he was able to make a cop cool. He had a cool name, cool car, cool clothes, a gorgeous girlfriend, a confident roguish attitude that never listened to authority or agendas, only to those hip to what's happening now.

After *Bullitt* was released Neile said, "During interviews, Steve talked a lot about one's dignity as an actor, the dignity of the filmmaker, and his dignity as a human being." Steve said, "I've got a feeling I'm leaving stardom behind, you know. I'm gradually becoming more of a filmmaker, acquiring a different kind of dignity from that which you achieve in acting." The success also gave validity to Steve's production company Solar and the next three films he would make were passion projects and art films. In 2007 *Bullitt* was preserved in the United States National Film Registry by the Library of Congress for its cultural and historical significance. The film would be McQueen's most iconic film and was his fifth box office success in a row.

The Getaway
1972

"Insecurity is pretty good motivation." -Steve McQueen

Steve McQueen was on top of the world when *Bullitt* came out but his next three films were financial failures. His return to comedy in *The Reivers* failed to find an audience or laughs. Steve's dream project *Le Mans* was a complete disaster in the American market and during production he lost his agent, his assistant, his company Solar, his working relationship with John Sterges, his marriage, and he hit his midlife crises. Then Steve's next film *Junior Bonner*, a modern day western, was also a financial failure.

After three heavy failures Steve wanted to make his comeback into the action genre with his next film. He signed a three film deal with First Artist where he was given creative control and 10-15% of the profits. Once the papers were signed everything started falling into place. Steve's publicist turned producer David Foster said, "For years, I'd been bugging Steve to play an out-and-out gangster—you know, a ruthless, cold, but ultimately redeeming baddie." The gangster they were looking for was Doc McCoy in the script for *The Getaway*.

Talent agent Mike Medavoy said, "I knew Steve had always wanted to play a real Bogart character—a lovable crook—and when I saw *The Getaway*, I said, 'Wow. This is it!" He sent a copy to Steve who quickly responded: "Lock it up." David Foster then went after a director to attach to the film, "I went to Peckinpah on the idea with my heart in my throat, prepared to hype him 'til kingdom come, if necessary. Right away, he said, 'I know the story cold, for Christ's sake. I'll do it." Turns out Sam Peckinpah had been trying to make the movie ten years earlier and loved the idea of doing the film with Steve.

"Of course to do one picture with Steve you must be a

117

little crazy," Peckinpah said adding, "To do two you must be absolutely mad. So three would make me completely insane. He's a beautiful guy to work with, a dedicated actor, we both worked toward the same end. He's a very creative man and I enjoy working with creative people who have ideas."

"[McQueen] wanted to be as real as anybody could possibly be real in everything that he played." -Robert Vaughn

In preparation for his role in *The Getaway*, Steve spent time working in real prison shops including a textile mill, license plate factory, and he even cut brush with prisoners along roads. "I sorta lived with them, inmates, for about a week and a half," Steve said. "I didn't sleep there but I was with them all day. And the order the guards had was to treat me like any other inmate. And I got yelled at and screamed at and ran everywhere I went. I tell Ya, a lot of those guys were there for murder, a lot of them were there for severe crimes."

Many people incorrectly assume that this type of preparation is "Method Acting," but to most actors, this is simply doing their homework. Steve was not trying to become the character of Doc and change his way of thinking to that of a prisoner. Steve was simply obtaining better familiarity with the tasks he would have to engage in on camera so he could look as authentic as possible. The beginning of the film was filmed in a real Texas correctional facility with real prisoners around him at all times. Steve knew if he wasn't completely authentic he would stand out in a negative way so that the magic of cinema would be lost on the audience.

Because of Steve's dedication and preparation he gave a flawless portrayal of a prisoner. Steve was so authentic that once after the Peckinpah yelled "cut" and Steve began to walk off the work detail he was chased down by guard dogs.

Except for his films *Hell Is For Heroes* and *The War Lover*, Steve portrayed himself in his roles rather than adopting what he perceived his character to be. This played to his strong suits and made him the star he was. For this film, Steve tried something entirely new saying, "We all decided the look of the picture and the feel of the picture should be what *High Serra* had. I sort of fashion in a way what I'm playing here after Bogart, which I've never done before. I did it in a way because, I guess it's a tribute, for all of us. Walter Hill dedicated the picture to Raoul Walsh I think because of his direction in *High Sierra*. That picture was one of my favorites, and one of Sam Peckinpah's favorites."

According to his wife, while they were dating, Steve never missed a Bogart film. "I first saw Bogart on the screen when I was a kid," Steve said. "He nailed me pronto, and I've admired him ever since. He was the master and always will be." Steve studied Humphrey Bogart's character in the 1941 film *High Sierra*. Watching the film over and over and adopting what was appropriate for his own role in *The Getaway*. He styled his hair after Bogie and even had the wardrobe department make him a similar suit to the one Bogart wore in the film. Steve didn't just copy Bogart however, he made these things his own.

"Steve was totally careful about realism," said David Foster. "I couldn't believe the weeks he put in wardrobe and the weapons. He had a very strong fix on what he wanted Doc to look like. Back in the early seventies, prisoners' heads were shaved. He wanted to have a bowl cut so that the rest of the film, he wouldn't have to get his hair cut. On screen, his hair kept growing and growing. It started one way and filled in later on. It was a small touch, but it was his idea." And as for his suit, Steve requested that his suit not be perfect and have the cuffs of his pants to be tattered, he reasoned that a convict is not the type of person to have a tailor.

"It's going to be difficult for me. I usually play the Peter Perfect man." -Steve McQueen

When Steve chose to model his role on Humphrey Bogart he had a very colorful character to draw from. Bogart himself was a man with a lisp, a scar on his face, rug on his head, yet this tough looking man was born on Christmas Day, and his on screen persona mirrored all these traits. He was one of the first silver screen bad guys that audiences sympathized with because as tough as he was and as mean as he looked he had a face that radiated a complicated inner life showing that he could be hurt. The dichotomy doesn't stop there, in *Casablanca,* Bogart says, "I stick my neck out for nobody," and at the same time he's sticking his neck way out to help his friends, a common theme in many of his films.

Humphrey Bogart often plays characters who want a fair deal, keep their cool under pressure, and yet are just as harsh as the world around them. In the same vein, Bogart knows he's had a hard life and wants better for those he cares about, often trying to shield the "dames" from the dog-eat-dog reality of the world they live in. Between his thousand yard stares and his cloaked passion Bogart's roles consists of a fine balancing act. Steve was able to emulate Bogart's character without falling into the realm of caricature by making clear and specific choices.

Steve emulated Bogart by giving Doc a crooks code of ethics. In one scene he finally catches up to a guy who stole his half million dollars and has the courtesy to tell the thief "When you work on a lock, don't leave any scratches." Before knocking the guy unconscious. What Steve brings to the scene is a sense of empathy for the low time crook.

Steve brings sympathy in another scene when he chooses not to kill one of the main antagonists Rudy who's lying unconscious. As laid out in the script he raises his gun point blank range to Rudy's head, chooses not to shoot then lowers the gun. A specific nuance that adds to his character is Steve's choice to raise his other hand to shield himself from any blood splatter before choosing not to kill Rudy. This adds to the chilling realism that Doc has executed people like this in the past. In these scenes, Steve was able to bring empathy to an assault scene and brutality to a sympathetic scene adding to the Bogart-like dichotomy of his role.

Steve trusted his instincts when making specific choices concerning his role and he also trusted them with his camera technique. The greatest acting in the world is thrown away if the actor doesn't play towards the camera. One of the makeup artists on *The Getaway* didn't get what the big fuss was about Steve, "I watched him act closely on the set of *The Getaway* one day and after they filmed this particular scene, I went to the director Sam Peckinpah and said, 'I don't get it; he doesn't look like he is doing anything.' So Sam got me to sit right under the camera one day when we were in a very tight set and said, 'Watch now, and then we will see dailies.' Again I didn't see him do much while sitting almost right in front of him. But when I went to dailies it was all there. He had an incredible magic between the camera and himself that the naked eye didn't see."

Steve's reactions were so subtle that only the magnification of the camera lens could see them. He was a true cinematic actor and the camera was his greatest tool. "Watching him perform was a trip," actress Barbara Leigh said. "Steve's approach to acting was different than most, and that's what separated him from most movie stars. He was a reactor instead of an actor. He didn't initiate action; he reacted with his facial expressions and body language. Most actors fight for lines; Steve fought for the shot. Where he placed himself was more important to him than what he had to say. He didn't appear to be acting at all, but that was his gift."

Since his days of studying himself on *Wanted: Dead or Alive* Steve picked up on the intimacies of the camera and knew just how to take advantage of them. Peckinpah said, "If you really want to learn about acting for the screen watch McQueen's eyes." Often when actors walk into a new room during a scene their eyes will dart quickly across the room looking at everything giving them a panicked feeling. Steve, on the other hand, will pick a specific point in the room to focus on, in a beat he'll process the information and form an opinion before moving onto the next point. Similarly, Steve always makes eye contact before initiating physical contact. For example, he'll look at his wife's lips before kissing her. Steve does this with people and objects and this simple tactic means that nothing he does feels unwarranted.

Through his eye's alone Steve could convey that he was striving to do something, which makes his performances so riveting. David Foster said, "When reading the script, [Steve] would flip right through it and say, 'Too many words, too many words. I'll give you a close-up that'll say a thousand words.' That was him. He would give you one big smile and save you three pages of dialogue. He didn't think a convict would be very erudite or have long speeches, and he was correct. The whole film was like that."

Watching actors strive to do something is what audiences pay to see even if that something is as common as making breakfast. Steve felt that the film needed a scene dealing with the morning after he's gotten out of jail and his wife have made love for the first time since. Steve took on the task of writing the new scene himself and when he was done he had written seven pages of dialogue. When Sam said that they would film the scene Steve's eyes lit up he was so excited.

Steve isn't just cooking breakfast, he's striving to cook the greatest breakfast of all time to show his wife he appreciates her. He's cooking several things at once on the stove top, swashing food around, and drinking a beer. He's being playful and messy, here the 'King of Cool' is even whistling and talking to himself! Then his wife comes in he transitions to giving her all his attention letting the food burn and smoke fill the room. The cooking loses importance, they embrace and the one minute scene ends with only a few words spoken between them.

The next day after they watched the dailies Sam said to Steve, "And that was what you wrote seven pages of dialogue to explain?" Steve laughed as he responded, "Well, you know better than to listen to me, Sam." Even though the scene goes by quickly Steve was able to convey everything that had taken him seven pages of dialogue heavy writing to explain.

Ali MacGraw who was playing his wife and ended up marrying Steve after they wrapped shooting said, "He's a great great great film actor I think. He's just, I can't think of very many actors anywhere that are as interesting to watch as he is. I mean his mistakes are interesting to watch. I think he has wonderful instincts and great presence. He's one of the few movie actors that I would like to watch anything of. You know I don't think it really matters what it really is I think his presence is enough. It's a funny thing but occasionally I get terrified finding myself across the camera from him. I think, you know because I have not worked a lot and every once in a while I look up and lose track of the job I'm doing and realize that it's Steve McQueen and almost have a heart attack."

"Lawyers sharpen up with law books, and astronauts in pressure chambers, but an actor has to do it the way a prize fighter does." -Steve McQueen

Steve McQueen was an actor who understood how to do the specifics of his job and when he wasn't filming he was constantly training. For many actors, this training would consist of going to acting classes or doing theater. But for Steve acting consisted of making actions believable so he did his training in the gym, the race track, the martial arts dojo, and the gun range.

For *The Getaway*, much of Steve's authenticity depended on his physical ability and familiarity with firearms. Steve first received proper firearm training in the Marine Corps where he was trained on all light infantry weapons. He learned how to safely handle, disassemble, clean, reassemble, load, and shoot accurately under all weather conditions. Steve proved to be a natural and was given sharp shooter status with the M-1 Garand rifle and the Colt M1911A1 automatic pistol, which he uses as his main sidearm in the film.

Peckinpah was so comfortable with Steve's ability that there were full loads and real bullets in the guns for the most of his shooting scenes. Walter Hill, the film's screenwriter said, "I don't think anybody ever handled guns as well in movies. You see Steve's military training in his films. He was so brisk and confident in the way he handled guns. It was a very fresh approach in its time."

In the early seventies, James Bond was still firing his tiny pistol randomly from the hip when Steve McQueen was carefully aiming down the sights of his 45 and this did more than give McQueen authenticity. From a film making perspective, guns create heavily emphasized lines. When the guns are aimed correctly these lines of action are visually pleasing and even when static they create an illusion of movement like racing stripes on a parked car.

When Steve looks through the sights down the barrel of a gun the energy he is exuding through his face travels down the sight radius and he is expressing direction with energy, the gun becomes an extension of his intentions. When an actor doesn't know what they're doing and holds a pistol down by the hips (like James Bond) or with a bent wrist (like Rick Grimes on *The Walking Dead*) there is no clear line of direction and a storytelling element has been neglected.

Steve didn't just practice with guns for his films but supported his second amendment rights to keep and bear arms. Even years later when Steve married Barbra Minty the two of them and Steve's little step son Joshua would go out to the Malibu hills for target practice. "Steve's military training in the late 1940s stuck with him for the rest of his life and he was very proficient with weapons of all kinds - pistols, handguns, rifles, and shotguns. He knew how to field strip a weapon blindfolded and expected me to do it as well. We even had an escape plan in case an intruder broke into the house," said Barbra. "Steve wanted me to be ready for a combat situation. Guess that's why he kicked ass in all of his movies."

Steve's interest in guns wasn't the only thing informing his acting, he was also practicing martial arts. In the beginning, there was really only one martial arts teacher that was teaching the classical material to non-orientals and that was Bruce Lee. Bruce's other celebrity students included James Garner, Roman Polanski, and James Coburn. Steve had met Bruce before Bruce worked on *The Green Hornet* and the two would eventually train together and become friendly rivals, Bruce calling himself the "Oriental Steve McQueen."

Eventually, Bruce left California for Hong Kong and got his film career off the ground. Steve needed a new trainer so Bruce recommended another would be legend, "If you ever want to take karate lessons, Norris is the best."

Steve trained with Chuck Norris until Norris's career started taking off so Steve then trained with Chucks pupal and associate Pat E. Johnson who would become one of Steve's closest friends.

When Bruce Lee was asked which of his celebrity clientele was the best fighter he simply responded, "McQueen, that son of a gun, got the toughness in him." Pat had something similar to say, "Steve was probably the most aggressive guy I've ever, ever trained. He really wanted to get the martial arts so he could learn some self-discipline. He had an ego, no denying that at all, he had a real short fuse, he could go off in an instant, but he wanted to learn to control that temper as well as know how to fight so if somebody did get in his face, he'd be able to either walk away or know that he could put the guy out right now."

Steve's martial arts ability became another tool of authenticity he could bring to his roles. In the train sequence when he catches up to the thief who stole his half million he knocks the guy unconscious. Richard Bright the actor playing the thief recalls the beating he took, "Steve didn't hold anything back but he had perfect control. A lot of the new actors try to be more realistic, but they don't have control. Steve was a guy who mastered his power and knew how to use it. He would go all out, always putting safety first. I think mentally he would let go to find out everything he could possibly do, and in that sense, he was totally free. Physically, he was very principled guy. He could throw a slap with an eighteenth of an inch space between his hand and your face. He was extremely careful that it looked good and forceful I had no sense of him harming me physically. It was wonderful working with Steve."

Nowadays actors rarely do their own stunts and even have doubles who do their fighting for them. Even so with all the fast cuts, sound effects, and the heavy use of shaky cam, actors today with little physical ability can be given the illusion of being a good fighter, this wasn't the case for the action heroes of Steve's era.

"Steve and Sam had a strange relationship. Both knew just how far to push the other and the boundaries - they made it work." -Barbara Leigh

Steve was coming off three commercial flops and needed *The Getaway* to put him back on top so during post production he took control from Peckinpah. The deal Steve made with First Artist gave him creative control and along with that final cut. In the editing room, Steve was picking the shots of him that looked best and choosing to keep the camera on himself rather than cutting to the other actors. Peckinpah said, "McQueen's playing it safe, and that's going to be his downfall. He chose all these Playboy shots of himself. He's playing it safe with these pretty-boy shots."

The film was released just as Steve wanted, critics thought *The Getaway* was too violent and even Peckinpah wasn't pleased with the reaction the film got, "*The Getaway* was my first attempt at satire, badly done... To many people took it too seriously. Five times in that picture I have people saying, 'It's just a game.' I was dealing with a little bit of *High Sierra* there and a couple of other things. It was a good story, and I thought I had a good ending. It made my comment." Regardless of what critics thought audiences flocked to the film and *The Getaway* became the second highest grossing film of the year; McQueen was back on top.

Steve said after the film was released and became a success, "*The Getaway* meant more to me in a financial and professional way than *Junior Bonner*. I take full responsibility for it. Not full credit, but full responsibility. It's made money for everyone connected with it. That says all there is to say. I know Sam wasn't happy with some of the

127

changes, but I had my reasons. Sam and I are still friends. And, of course, personally, *The Getaway* was a film that I met my lady on. Ali and I had a chance to meet and get to know each other, so it has a sentimental value for me as well. I feel that Sam Peckinpah is an exceptional film-maker. He is a little bit hard on himself sometimes, and I worry about him for that but I have great respect for anyone as committed as Sam is to his work. He surrounds himself with people who are honest and who are personally committed to what he does. Sam makes a personal commitment to his work and I feel that a man isn't worth a shit unless he has."

Peckinpah in return respected McQueen saying, "We fought all the time. I never met an actor - a good actor - that I didn't fight with. And McQueen was one of the best. He was very, very under-rated. He was very tough, very, very, very good."

Papillon
1973

"I'm tired of being the Chief. I just want to be an indian. I'm going to concentrate for a while on being an actor." -Steve McQueen

McQueen was hugely popular in France in 1973 where his TV series *Wanted Dead or Alive* was aired long after the show's cancellation. So his French fans loved hearing he would be portraying the real life Frenchmen Henri Charrière. Henri who was nicknamed Papillon for the butterfly tattoo on his chest was given a life sentence and ten years hard labor after he was wrongfully convicted of murdering a pimp. He was then transported to a penal colony in French Guiana where he was put in a labor camp and eventually sent to Devil's Island.

Along with hard labor, Papillon would spend several years in solitary confinement where he was deprived of light and nutrition as well as endured attempts by the guards to dehumanize him. Throughout all of this torment, Papillon was able to keep his spirits up and eventually escape to freedom.

When asked about picking roles Steve said, "I do it by instinct. But I have to be careful because I'm a limited actor. I mean, my range isn't very great. There's a whole lot of stuff I can't do, so I have to find character and situation that feel right. Even then, when I've got something that fits, it's a hell of a lot of work."

For someone who thinks they're a "limited actor" Steve sure picked a tough role and Papillon was without a doubt the most complex of his career. He would have to age 12 years and adopt a physical manner in balance with the tribulations that the role required. Despite all of this Steve was perhaps most worried about having to dawn a French accent and looked to his wife for advice. "My argument had been if all the actors involved spoke the same way, with no accents, and only alluded to themselves as Frenchmen, then problems wouldn't arise insofar as the public's accepting them in general, and Steve, as Henri Charrière, in particular."

In the end, having all the actors ignore the accents is precisely what they did and doing so doesn't take anything away from the film. Still, with all the complexities of the role, Steve decided he didn't want any part of the behind the scenes production and hired himself out solely as an actor saying, "Let the producer do his thing. I'll just act this time around."

The film was based on the book *Papillon* written by Henri Charrière himself and the screenplay was penned by two time Academy award winner (and black list victim) Dalton Trumbo. Trumbo was brought on after Director Franklin Schaffner tossed out the original script a few days before the production settled for shooting in Jamaica. They started filming with only 60 pages of script and Trumbo was able to stay about ten pages ahead of the filming schedule.

"When we began shooting, we didn't have a complete script," said Schaffner. "So with a few exceptions, we decided to shoot the entire film in sequence. The other factor in that decision was that the story covers 12 long, hard years, and the main characters clearly show the erosive effects. We felt that we could avoid many problems of makeup detail by filming in sequence."

Franklin Schaffner was no amateur director and previously directed *Planet of the Apes* and then won the Academy Award for his direction on *Patton*. The film's director of photography Fred Koenekamp loved Schaffner, "He was the best director that I ever worked with and he got on well with Steve, too. Frank was an easy guy to get along with; he never yelled on a set, he never pushed people, he knew exactly what he wanted and was always totally prepared, so I think he made it easy on actors. He'd chit-chat, talk about a scene, rehearse it and that would be it — he never became nasty."

Robert Swink was the films editor and three time Oscar nominee also saw the positive relationship between director and star, "He and Steve became quite close. The great thing about Frank was that you could go to him and say, 'Why don't you shoot from this angle or that angle?' He would listen and be prepared to use ideas from others. He was not proud and never out to get praise, and I think Steve recognized that humility."

"[McQueen] always played with such mystery, he had such a reserve to him and he had this emotional underpinning keeping you, the viewer, involved with what he was doing." -Pierce Brosnan

Steve was about to film the most challenging role of his life. He'd be playing a real living person and with a script that wasn't close to being finished but he found common ground with Papillon to jump off from. "I kept being driven by this restless feeling," Steve said. "I seemed always to be looking for something--never knowing what it was--but always there was the sense that I couldn't be confined. And that's exactly what I felt in common with Charrière's Papillon. This man, who had been restless and moving, suddenly found himself imprisoned, and his natural behavior and involuntary reaction was, 'I must get out of the damned place.' Of course, the kind of inhuman, brutalizing treatment practiced in the French penal colonies in those days added to his desire to be free. My name could easily have been Papillon, too."

Steve pulled the character of Papillon from himself rather than create something from nothing. "He was one of those natural actors like Gregory Peck - who I worked with on a few pictures - who were not in the same echelon as actors like Laurence Olivier or Frederic March," said Swink.

But calling Steve a "natural actor" doesn't mean he played himself either. Emanuel L. Wolf who was the executive producer on *Papillon* said, "Steve McQueen was a very intense man. He would never let anything go by casually. When you were with him you felt that intense, driven nature but he also had this wonderful charisma. I rarely saw him relax, but once the camera went on he became this cool guy. There was a switch in personality. But he had a wonderful personality for the screen that came out so wonderfully. It was such a strange dichotomy between the two characters: the Steve McQueen you worked with and met and talked with, and the Steve McQueen that you saw on the screen. They were two different people. And that made it difficult because I never quite knew which Steve I was dealing with. I've heard people say that he played himself, but in real life, I never saw in front of me the guy who's on the screen."

This film was also a gamble for Steve because *Papillon* is unlike his previousness successes in that there's no big battles, shootouts, or fast paced chase scenes to hook the audience. *Papillon* had more in common with a character piece than the action blockbuster Steve excelled at and what audiences expected to see in a Steve McQueen movie.

"If a guy like [Dustin Hoffman] can become a star, what'll happen to guys like Newman and me?" -Steve McQueen

Further separating this film from an action movie was the casting of Dustin Hoffman as Louis Dega, Papillon's main companion in the film. Dustin who was once considered the least likely to succeed by his acting class was taking Hollywood by storm being nominated by the Academy for the Best Actor in both *The Graduate* in 1967 and *Midnight Cowboy* in 1969.

Dustin and Steve are two completely different actors with two totally different approaches to the craft. Both had studied at the Actors Studio but that technique resonated with Hoffman and never did with McQueen. Their difference in craft is easily seen in their approaches to their physical appearance. Throughout the film, both men appear to be losing considerable weight despite their different approaches. Dustin was eating only one-half to one full coconut a day whereas Steve bypassed losing weight altogether. Instead he had the wardrobe department get him baggier clothing throughout production making his physique appear to shrink.

The director also recognized differences between his stars when they were in the process of filming and he found a way to work with their differences. "I would always shoot on McQueen first to make him commit and then turn around and shoot on Hoffman. It seemed to work better that way because if I covered Hoffman first, Steve would become restless about what he was doing. The quicker you got him comfortable, the better the scene would play. Hoffman, on the other hand, is totally electric performer. He comes in with 99 different ideas of how to approach a scene."

There are stories of Steve and Dustin not getting along on set but Koenekamp disagrees, "As a cameraman, you can't get any closer to the actors and I felt things couldn't have gone any smoother. I give Dustin a lot of credit because he's such a good actor; I feel he brought a lot out of Steve. When Steve and Dustin wanted to talk about something in the picture, they would get together in the evening and meet at Frank's house - that wasn't unusual. Like Steve, Dustin was also strong-minded who had his own ideas about the film too, which helped Steve to work harder. It was real healthy competition and they pushed each other to great heights."

Not since the *Cincinnati Kid* and Eddie Robinson had Steve worked with a big name Oscar nominated actor and watching Steve act alongside Dustin shows just how good of an actor Steve was. Don Gordon who played opposite Steve in *Bullitt* and who played Julot in this film said, "Steve worked hard on *Papillon*. He worked very hard as an actor, a lot of people think he didn't, but he did. He was a working actor. Plus the fact that Dustin Hoffman kept McQueen on his toes, kept him honest. One day Dustin showed up with his teeth all colored and wearing Coke-bottle glasses. McQueen had to be aware; he had to work even harder than he normally did. He really came to maturity on *Papillon*."

Dustin didn't just show up with colored teeth and funny looking glasses, he was trying to steal the movie away from Steve just like Steve stole *The Magnificent Seven* from Yul Brynner. Throughout the film, Dusty goes through five different pairs of glasses and wears six funny little hats he interchanges throughout the movie. He also shaved parts of his head to appear like he was balding. Dustin was doing everything he could to try and out McQueen McQueen, using Steve's old tricks.

"There was this young guy who was virtually growling, but I think Steve saw it as a kind of game," Gordon said. "A lot of people want to get serious about this crap, but though acting is serious business, it's not brain surgery, you're not saving somebody's life - you're acting. You should have a good time at it, work hard at it and be serious about it - Steve was all those things, but he also had a sense of fun. He saw Dustin for what he was - a young actor trying to make his way in the world. Anyone that says he saw him as a threat has got to be kidding as McQueen was never threatened by anybody."

Dusty was constantly coming up with things to steal the audience's attention away from Steve while Steve kept his antics to a minimum. Steve often left the top buttons of his shirt undone so that his butterfly tattoo would be visible and he took a lesson from Eli Wallach as his wife explained, "Ever since Steve had seen Eli Wallach wear a gold tooth as an extension of his character in *The Magnificent Seven*, Steve couldn't wait for the day when he'd be able to do the same. *Papillon* gave him the chance. He thanked his lucky stars he had remembered the gold tooth as soon as Dustin Hoffman walked onto the set with his little wire glasses. Steve never did take kindly to being bested, even by a little prop."

Steve had his own gold tooth made to wear but even this is not scene stealing, he's merely bringing the role to life. "I've cut everything down," Steve said. "Now I think of Laurence Olivier when he goes to work. He's got a little black bag with a couple of fake noses, his wig, or whatever he's got in there. And that's all I need--a pencil, a script, and a briefcase."

Steve no longer needed to go the extra distance to steal a scene, the pauses in his sentences were enough as he simply captured the audience's attention without the antics of his younger years. In Gary Oldman's words, "[McQueen] walks onto the screen and he kidnaps you."

Executive producer Emanuel Wolf said Dustin started viewing the dailies for an hour to two every night studying what they had shot. The film's editor was always watching the dailies too, "Dustin Hoffman used to come into the projection room, usually before everyone else arrived, and look at the rushes every night. He and I would sit and talk about the film. I can remember him saying, 'I can't get the upper hand on Steve, I always try, but all he has to do is blink his eyes or scratch his ear and he takes the scene from me.'" Editor Swink also added that he doesn't remember Steve ever going in to view the dailies, an uncommon move by Steve that really shows the confidence he was gaining as an actor.

Actor LeVar Burton noted, "By the time Steve did *Papillon*, it was a master-class. He went toe to toe with

Dustin Hoffman, who was kicking butt, but Steve was right there in every frame. Steve was brilliant in *Papillon.* You couldn't get the better of Steve, he would out-honest you!"

At times during filming, Steve offered Dustin some acting advice that he had learned over the years telling him, "Less Dusty. Do less. Just throw that out, you don't need it. Keep it simple." Years later when Dustin was doing Tootsie he revealed that he did, in fact, listen to Steve's advice.

Koenekamp noted they got along really well and were professional to each other and that's because they needed to be. "Both of us were suspicious; both of us wanted to come out of this multimillion-dollar film as career survivors," Dusty said. "Both of us realized we needed each other's help and support. I can't really speak for him, but I believe he was thinking the same thing. In the movie, one character is saying, 'You've got to help me or die; neither of us can do it alone'. And for us as the actors, the meaning is, 'We'd better help each other, or we could die with this movie."

"If you're going to do a part, you've got to excel at everything." -Steve McQueen

Years before while Steve was serving in the Marines he was sentenced to 42 days in the brig for going AWOL. Steve could have channeled his real life experience into his *Papillon* scenes through the different acting techniques he learned while studying with the masters in New York. Sanford Meisner, Uta Hagen, and Lee Strasberg each would have taught Steve a different way to use this experience in his art to achieve authenticity; however, no information has come to light that says he did go about using his past experiences here for emotional preparation. Physical preparation, on the other hand, is something Steve always did in his work.

In *Papillon* Steve had to recognize and translate how years of hard labor and solitary confinement changes a person physically. In the Meisner technique that Steve learned at The Neighborhood Playhouse these challenges are seen as character work as they force an actor to change something about his or herself.

Specifically for this film, Steve had to adopt several impediments. Impediments are just that, something that impedes normality such as making physical changes about movement or voice. For Steve in this film most the impediments he chose involved physical disabilities.

Steve honored the real Papillon through a long period of training. He began walking with a limp, talking differently, and other things that impede how Steve normally acts until those things become second nature. Hard work on physicality isn't new for Steve, on his racing film *Le Mans* two year earlier Steve practiced getting and out of his Porsche for six hours straight. Bob Rosen the film's production manager who caught Steve doing this recalled, "He wanted it to look normal to him. He felt if he looked awkward getting into a race car, the audience would somehow know."

In *Papillon*, the first of Steve's impediments do not show up in the film until he is put into solitary confinement and they didn't come out of nowhere either. When Papillon enters his concrete cell he displays his defiance. He makes the conscious choice to not let the system beat him down by exercising, brushing his teeth, and by crushing up bugs to put in his soup for nourishment. He tells himself over and over in a whisper, "I'm gonna be fine, I'm gonna be fine." But after two years with six months of being put on half rations in total darkness Papillon's body begins to decay.

Steve interprets this decay through his impediments. His face looks like someone just got up from a night with little rest, his eyes are sensitive to light and his body is stiff, his movements are small and jerky, his reactions are

137

slow and his voice is hoarse. When Papillon is finally released from solitary confinement and put back in with the other prisoners he has a raspy voice with a slow speech, his eyes seem to stare at nothing, and he has head to toe body movements with hunched shoulders and he moves as little as possible. Papillon's time spent in the infirmary shows him beginning to recover and Steve does this by slowly dialing back the impediments over the course of a few scenes until he's back to normal showing Papillon's full recovery.

"When I think of McQueen as an actor, I'm reminded of a star who embodied a certain mythology and brought it to life." -Anthony Zerbe

Anthony Zerbe had a small role in the film but was involved in one of the films greatest moments that tested Papillon and even Steve as an actor. "In our scene together, I played a leper in a French colony who could help Papillon escape to freedom. As a test, I offered him a cigar that had already been smoked, and McQueen's character did not know whether I was infectious or not. The cool thing was, I had been chewing on that cigar all day, and I handed him this wet, drooled on, soggy stogie. This was intentional because I wanted to see what that fucker was made of. It was obviously a challenge. McQueen, the actor, didn't have to take the cigar. He could have asked for a replacement during a cut but didn't. McQueen just put it in his mouth and continued with the scene. He delivered one of the most amazing reactions I have ever seen on the silver screen. Once the scene was over, I looked at him and said, 'Oh McQueen, you're something else.' He just looked at me and smiled. I thought it was an incredible thing to do and showed how far he was willing to go to bring respect to the part."

In order to make this scene, believable Steve didn't

have to believe that the cigar could give him leprosy because belief is not the job of the actor but of the audience. If an actor is real and doesn't try to add or ignore/suppress stimuli than the audience will believe in whatever the actor is doing because they have been given no reason not to believe. An actors belief that he is truly in the situation is simply not required or needed. Because Steve does nothing false he is believable, the greatest acting trick he ever used was that he knew he was acting. What the audience sees is Papillon's hesitation in not wanting to take the possibly infected cigar into his mouth but in reality, the reaction came from Steve not wanting to take the slobbery cigar.

Once Papillon escapes and is captured again he spends another five years in solitary confinement and for the rest of the film, he has a new set of impediments that are a little more extreme having spent more time in the concrete box. His neck and back are rigid, his eyes continuously squinting, he has a hoarse voice, and an odd walk.

The last of Steve's impediments was one he picked up on the fly, "I felt Charrière should have some kind of physical handicap when he is finally released after five years of solitary confinement. I kept looking for some type of inspiration. Then I watched Franklin Schaffner walk. He walked with a limp. I just copied him and that's how Papillon developed his limp."

Don Gordon noted, "All of that work for him was very tough. He just busted his ass. He worked. That's what he did. Forget about him being a star, he was an actor. He did his part better than any other actor in the world who could have done *Papillon*. He brought to it another dimension." Koenekamp also said about his work ethic, "I think he probably worked harder as an actor than he'd ever done before. It was a very demanding role, particularly towards the end of the picture when he is an old man."

"He was very proud of his work in *Papillon* and not many people realize that. He worked very hard and very seriously at his craft; McQueen poured a lot of himself into that film." -Don Gordon

Papillon would become the fourth highest earning film of 1973 and the most successful film ever made by Allied Artists. And with this film, Steve became the highest paid actor in the world when he received his 2 million up front.

Steve felt this was his best performance which was recognized and nominated for a Golden Globe Award for Best Motion Picture Actor - Drama. *Papillon* won an Oscar for best original score but that's the only Academy award nomination the film got.

Producer Emanuel Wolf said, "Whatever anyone might say about Steve, he and Dustin on this movie were pretty marvelous and should have received more recognition. Part of the reason was the antagonism that Steve had built up among the Academy members. Steve was not all that popular in some circles."

Steve had given a performance that should have won him an Oscar but the Academy didn't even nominate him. McQueen is most remembered for being so damn cool rather than his acting ability for surely every great actor has won an Academy Award, right? Perhaps Steve would have been remembered differently if he had won but the truth is he upset too many people in the industry has fought his way to the top.

Steve will always be a legend and as Pat Johnson said "Acting styles go through changes and Steve was a man who was so ahead of his time. Actors are now taking a cue from him. The trend is now going back to honesty. Steve's influence was all over these kids."

Tom Horn
1980

"You only go around once in life and I'm going to grab a
handful of it." -Steve McQueen

In the seven years that passed between *Papillon* and
the making of *Tom Horn*, Steve McQueen went through
many changes in his life. His fame reached a peak with
the success of his film *The Towering Inferno* the highest
grossing film of 1974. But after this success, Steve lost his
interest in doing films and being a movie star.

He fought for so many years to get to the top of the
industry and when he got there his priorities in life shifted.
For two years Steve chose not to work, turning down all
the roles offered to him including classic films like *One
Flew Over the Cuckoo's Nest* and *Close Encounters of the
Third Kind*, as well as Rambo in *First Blood* and two
different roles in Francis Ford Coppola's *Apocalypse Now*.

Outside of leaving his film career the McQueen/
MacGraw divorce broke up Hollywoods number one
power couple and Steve met a young girl more at home
on a ranch than on the red carpet. "Steve McQueen was
47 years old when we first met," said Barbra Minty
McQueen. "He rode motorcycles, drank Old Milwaukee
beer, wore grungy clothes and flouted traditions. He had
tired of Hollywood and wanted to scale back his visibility.
He had not only conquered the mountain but had stayed
on top for years with classic films such as *The Magnificent
Seven*, *The Great Escape*, *The Cincinnati Kid*, *The Sand
Pebbles*, *The Thomas Crown Affair*, *Bullitt*, *The Getaway*,
and *Papillon*.

After he made 14.5 million on the blockbuster film *The
Towering Inferno* Steve stopped making movies for a few
years. He grew a beard, let his trademark blond locks
grow long, and dressed like a long-distance trucker. He
enjoyed driving funky old trucks, preferred greasy spoons

over trendy Los Angeles restaurants, collected motorcycles and toys and flew antique planes."

For Steve's return to film, he brought his new outlook on life to the work. Instead of continuing to build his fame he opted to do a film based on a classic Ibsen play stating, "I wanted to do *An Enemy of the People* because I wanted to do something pure. I wanted to do this play about a little guy who was being dumped on but who still believed."

The film was a failure and Warner Brothers actually shelved the film for several years. The failure hurt Steve deeply but in doing *An Enemy of the People* his enthusiasm for film and the craft of acting came back as he told the director "For the first time in my life, I really feel like I'm acting. You know, this really is the most exciting business in the world."

"At this stage in my life, I don't want to make ordinary movies anymore. If I can't make movies above average in quality, I'd rather take it easy. I wanted to do something I'd be proud of." -Steve McQueen

After *An Enemy of the People*, Steve tried to make film adaptations of Samuel Beckett's *Waiting for Godot* then *Old Times* by Harold Pinter but both projects failed to get off the ground. Running out of ideas Steve turned to an autobiography, *Life of Tom Horn, Government Scout and Interpreter*, "I've always wanted to do Horn's story; now it's just a matter of doing it a little sooner than I expected."

Tom Horn's story, like Steve's story, is one of a runaway farm boy who lived a life of adventure. Horn became a scout and interpreter during the bloody Apache Wars playing a big part in the surrender of Geronimo while gaining the respect of his peers and rising through the ranks. When the war ended he built a ranch only to have his entire stock of 100 cattle and 26 horses stolen one night causing him to go bankrupt. He then became a range detective and dedicated his life to killing cattle rustlers.

Horn's personal vendetta brought him into many American conflicts in the old west like the Pleasant Valley War, Johnson County War, the Colorado Range War, and he even pursued Butch Cassidy's Wild Bunch gang. Then the Spanish American War broke out and he fought alongside Theodore Roosevelt's Rough Riders during their assault on San Juan Hill. When the war ended he returned to the West as a hired gun and range detective, that's when he was accused of murdering a 14-year-old boy and sentenced to death by hanging.

Associate producer Phil Parslow made the connection that at the end of Horn's life "Time had passed him by. The Indians were gone, the West was gone. He was born on the cusp. He started young and had outlived his time. In my mind, there's a lot of Tom Horn/Steve McQueen similarities. They both even died at fifty."

Fascinated by the life of Tom Horn, Steve became the films executive producer and began planning a 10 million dollar epic on the life of the man. Steve looked to Louis L'Amour, his favorite western novelist, to help him on the film. Louis turned the job down but invited Steve over to do research in his personal library of 17,000 books. Kathy L'Amour said, "Steve wanted to take the books home, but Louis wouldn't let him. So he'd come out to our house every day and read. Louis and I would be working in his office while Steve was sitting over on the sofa studying and making notes. That went on for weeks."

Making a film on the life of Tom Horn was possibly one of the film projects Steve was most passionate about in his life. Bud Shrake said, "He wanted to talk constantly about *Tom Horn* the movie in detail; he cared deeply about it. He had a vision of what he wanted it to be and look like. I think this might have been Steve's favorite movie. He had the book *The Life of Tom Horn* on him all the time and he had it memorized. I know he loved that movie."

Barbra said, "Despite all his previous success and accolades, I don't think he prepared any harder for a role than he did for *Tom Horn*. I still have more than 45 hours of conversations Steve held with writers, producers, directors, historians, and costumers associated with the movie."

Steve made these recordings to document the film making process. In one of the recordings, Steve made after reading a draft of the script he noted, "The whole introduction of Horn and Coble is wrong [...] it should be outside not inside. I somehow see it on the ranch to show the audience visually what kind of country we are talking about [...] this is where Horn looks best and is at ease."

The scene was changed and in fact, almost all of the film was shot during winter in Mescal, Arizona and most of that outdoors. Steve also noted in one of the recording that he disliked when Coble asked to see Horn's revered shooting skills saying, "I don't believe in any of this business [...] that's all horse shit that's been done a million times in movies and on television and I don't plan on doing that on this one." This part too was changed.

Steve's planned a four hour long epic on the life of Tom Horn but that was reduced in size over time as First Artists began reducing the budget from 10 million to eventually 3 million. Because of the budget cuts, Horn's more adventurous years were slowly cut from the film. And when production realized Geronimo had to be cut entirely from the film producer Fred Weintraub recalled, "Steve was okay about it; he didn't like it, but he understood the situation."

Thomas McGuane wrote the first draft then Bud Shrake was given the task of shortening the script, "When Steve gave me the script I thought it was going to be an easy job and just throw half of it away. But it wasn't that simple as McGuane had written scenes thirty pages long when they could have been three, so I had to do a rewrite, but using most of his original material."

In the end, both McGuane's script and Shrake's script were used in the film as well as drafts of the film that Steve penned once principle photography began.

"I have a feeling that I'm very well connected to this piece. I really feel this is my destiny to tell the true story of Tom Horn." -Steve McQueen

Barbra had been with McQueen from early on in the production and she got an in-depth look at his preparation process. "I believe the secret to Steve's success was that he began to learn about his character as soon as he signed on to do a film and continued to do so until the camera was ready to roll. Once the shooting started, Steve knew his character as well as he knew himself. As much as Steve would have liked the public to think that he didn't give a damn about acting, the truth is exactly the opposite — he cared very much about his craft. From what I witnessed, Steve wasn't a method actor. In fact, he frowned upon that approach. Instead, he started his research by reading all the material that he could get his hands on about the person, or the type of person he was going to play. He truly believed in presenting his character as honestly as possible, never wanting to make his acting produce a 'Hollywood' caricature or superhero. Realism was his driving force. 'God is in the details,' is what Steve would always say."

When Steve made *Bullitt*, he rode with a San Francisco police detective on actual cases. On *The Towering Inferno*, he fought alongside 200 firemen to put out a real nasty blaze on two sound stages at Goldwyn Studios. For

The Hunter, Steve not only read Christopher Keane's book on Ralph Thorson but spent many hours with the bounty hunter, picking his brains and finding out what made him tick.

Concerning his own acting, Steve said, "I try not to take myself too seriously. But at the same time, they pay me an awful lot of money to do my job, and I do everything I can to see that it's done right. I believe that today's audiences are smart and that you have the responsibility to articulate a part accurately. I mean, I don't look at it as play-acting. If I'm going to play a fireman, then for the period of that film--I am a fireman. For three months, or whatever, they own me, and I have a responsibility as a professional to do the best I can."

McQueen also demanded this level of professionalism from every member of the cast including the stuntmen he hired. According to actor Bert Williams, "He took all the stuntmen cowboys up to this ranch and had them ride; going through tests to make sure they weren't bullshitting him about the riding. He put them through a routine with his stunt coordinator. They had them jumping logs, going through roughage, going over rocks and at a hard pace, so if they were kidding as a rider they were going to be found out. Steve was that professional."

For *Tom Horn*, not only did Steve read everything there was on the man and the time period but he took things one step further. Steve and Barbra took a road trip to Boulder Colorado where they had a picnic at Horn's grave site. At the time Steve said, "I just wanna see if I can pick up on Horn's vibration." Later on, Steve expressed, "I could feel him under there. It was like he said to me, 'Please do my story. Please tell my story." And with that Steve threw everything he had into the film making process. McQueen researched and help write the script, was executive producer, star of the film, and if that wasn't enough he was about to add director to the list.

James William Guercio was the third director to come onto the project and he had only one credit to his name, a questionable one at that. Fred Weintraub openly said to Steve, "I'm completely against this man directing the film. He doesn't understand the movie business." And on the third day of filming Steve realized this himself and fired Guercio telling the cinematographer, "I don't think this is going to work out. I don't think he knows anything about the camera and real cinema and what we're trying to tell."

At this point, the film had gone through three directors and in the midst of shooting the film, Steve decided to direct the film himself. On set cowboy, Joe Brown said, "The film company didn't seem to be able to settle on who would direct the film, so Steve took it on himself to keep everybody moving. He made sure that company indecision did not waste any time. Filming happened on schedule. Steve and cinematographer John Alonzo brought the company together every morning before the first scene and kept it busy until it wrapped."

The Directors' Guild, however, got wind of this and because Steve wasn't a card-carrying member of the guild they found some silly rules to prevent him from taking over as the official director. But rather than waste time fighting the rules, Steve decided he would quickly hire a new director as a figurehead. William Wiard, who had only done TV shows like *The Rockford Files* and *M*A*S*H*, was hired as the film's director but that was only a title and he contributed very little to the filmmaking process. Reports from those on set said that for the most part Wiard stood around like a production assistant and enjoyed his paid vacation while Steve handled the directing with the help of cinematographer John Alonzo.

The facts remain consistent that Steve was a very capable director and co-star Bert Williams believed that he would have been one of the great directors had he lived long enough to direct more films. Steve had twenty years experience in the movie industry, a trained eye for what worked on camera, and with that an in-depth knowledge of every facet of the film making process. He needed all of that mastery on the set of *Tom Horn*, which was quickly becoming the most problematic of his career. Trying to keep the film on time and on budget meant being creative and having to make a lot of decisions on the fly. "Steve had both scripts in his hands when we were shooting," Alonzo said. "He would look at certain parts of both and decide which version we were going to shoot."

Like all good directors, McQueen had a strong vision of what he wanted and was able to effectively communicate that to his actors and get the best performances out of them. "On my first take as the Judge, I gave this great stage-like monologue while Tom Horn is up in court," said actor Bert Williams. "The extras, the crew, everyone applauded me, but Steve said, 'Bert, you're missing the point. You've got to remember that you're railroading me. You know it and I know it. Speak to me like a father speaks to his son, patronize me, and maybe spit out a bit of tobacco, that'll be a nice touch.' He really knew what he wanted. He was a good filmmaker and had a nice, low-key way of being powerful."

McQueen had come a long way from bullying directors on the set of *Wanted Dead or Alive* and was open to the suggestions of others, especially if the suggestion came from Alonzo. Assistant director Ed Milkovich noted, "He would listen to people and would sometimes change his thoughts in midstream. Like if cameraman John Alonzo said, 'Steve it would be better if we shot it this way,' Steve would say, 'Okay - I always listen to the cinema-photographer' as he called them."

"[McQueen's] a better actor than people think. His looks

148

and personality stamped him as a kind of macho sex symbol, but he's a whale of an actor, make no mistake about it." -Eli Wallach

Steve came off of his last two films with a new set of values that he brought to his acting craft. His youthful hunger was replaced with humility and Steve made the transition from movie star to movie actor where his celebrity appeal was replaced with the mark of a good story teller. "On *The Magnificent Seven*, he was a young and energetic star with a big ego, emotional about his position in the picture and jealous of Yul Brynner's fame. On *Tom Horn*, he was a very passionate man. He changed in the sense that he was more concerned for the other guy as opposed to himself," Alonzo said.

There were other changes too, Steve who had been so insecure about his height and image had loosened up and warmed up to the idea of aging on screen. "Now that Steve was closing in on 50, he wanted to act his age on screen and wanted a more 'adult' role," Barbra said.

McQueen had spent most of the last six years enjoying life and watching his kids grow, he was finding religion for the first time, and his need to be the worlds biggest star came to rest. Through *Tom Horn*, Steve was able to display exactly where he was at this stage in his life. Steve who had always portrayed characters constantly doing independent activities or striving to achieve something opens *Tom Horn* with a shot of him resting atop a grassy hill with his horse looking out at the sun set contemplating something unknown.

Previously the most important part of a Steve McQueen film was getting the chance to see Steve McQueen in action, something he had modeled after his favorite movie stars like James Cagney and Humphrey Bogart. But by the transition from movie star to movie actor; telling the story became the most important aspect of his films.

When the film opened in theaters Steve was asked why he made the film. Steve replied, "It's a film about a hero, and there are few left in this world." Being a hero had come to mean something different to Steve. He had never wanted to be the hero who swooped in and saved the day. Instead in films like *The Great Escape* he opted to be the hero without doing anything physically heroic, he was able to get around this conundrum by portraying a man simply doing his job and that to him was heroic. Now on *Tom Horn* being a hero meant not stooping down to the level of the "pasty-faced bunch of sheriffs" that ultimately hang him for a crime they know he didn't commit.

A valuable shift in the evolution of McQueen's acting craft came from his transition from acting derived from energy to acting derived from instinct. This is the difference of taking the script and planning out how the scene will go and instead trusting oneself to allow the actors instincts to take over once the scene is in play.

Even when memorizing his dialogue he didn't plan how he was going to deliver his lines, His wife said, "Many evenings we'd go over his lines for the next day. When Steve read them, I'd often laugh out loud, he sounded so stiff. Then he'd go in front of the camera and was magical."

Steve's first acting teacher Sanford Meisner said, "It takes twenty years to become a master." And with *Tom Horn*, Steve crossed the twenty-year mark and into acting mastery. The result of this is seen in the new creatively free and relaxed feature of his acting. Barbra Leigh who acted along Steve in *Junior Bonner* noted, "His power came from his facial expressions and his subtle body movements. Only the camera could capture the reality of his work. I remember watching Steve during the filming of the movie and thinking he wasn't acting. But, he most certainly was. Later when I saw the completed scenes I realized that he was a master of his craft." Steve had always been an actor who didn't appear to be acting but being relaxed on screen was something new entirely. James Coburn said, "*Tom Horn*, I thought was Steve's best film. He was loose and free and he wasn't guarded. Most of his films he was guarded. He had a form. If the film was rigid enough, he was going to be good. I always felt that Steve would really be a good actor if he ever grew up.... I think he finally did on *Tom Horn*. That was him finding his adulthood."

Steve was now more relaxed on screen but that didn't make him boring. If a scene wasn't too serious he would be quick to find humor in the situation like a normal person in real life, which added to his charisma. Being more relaxed also affected how he acted with his costars. Before, if an actor wasn't giving him much to work with, Steve would use a little extra effort to steal the scene one way or another, now Steve would use that extra effort to get more from the other actor and elevate their acting together. A good actor makes the other actors around him/her better by demanding the truth while they are in a scene together. If one of Steve's costars gives him only 25% then he would pull him up to 100% to match his level of realism.

By all accounts the older McQueen was wonderful to be on set with, a younger Steve McQueen would have been fighting for power, screen time, or recognition; but not on this film. He was still unapologetic about his behavior but now unchained of the need to prove his dominance.

Rob Goldman who was invited to the set noted, "McQueen's positive attitude and passion were infectious. His generosity to the cast and crew made them all want to give their best, and they took pride in pleasing him in a way that wasn't patronizing. It was interesting how Slim Pickens and McQueen joked between takes, talking about the good old days, but when the cameras started rolling,

McQueen was all business. Watching him come down the steps during his breakout in the jail scene and observing his facial expressions was something I'll never forget. I learned a lot about film acting that day and about McQueen the person as well." And Joe Brown an on set cowboy said, "Steve changed my opinion of actors. Generally, they entertain us and only have to ply their craft well to be admired. However, Steve passed on the special joy of adventure that he experienced in real life, and showed me that acting can be an adventure too."

"When I believe in something, I fight like hell for it." -Steve McQueen

With *Tom Horn*, Steve showed the world his talents as a well-rounded filmmaker. "He had a great visionary mind and a great story mind," costar Bert Williams said. So strong was Steve's vision that he almost scrapped the entire film during the editing process when his editor couldn't follow Steve's thought process.

Aside from multiple editors, the film went through, at least two writers (not including Steve) wrote full scripts, and four directors (not including Steve) were assigned to the film. After a 70% budget cut and three years of hard work, *Tom Horn* proved to be one of Steve's most problematic films but the problems didn't stop once the film was edited and ready for distribution. Alonzo explains, "Warners Didn't want it. It was just an obligation to First Artist, so they put as little money into it as possible. There was no promotion to the picture at all."

But after so many years of being away from the public, Steve's new film was well received by audiences and critics. *The Hollywood Reporter* wrote, "Steve McQueen, after a six-year absence, returns to the mainstream of filmmaking in a role that fits his persona like a well-worn saddle, as an Old West gunman who understands triggers but not trickery...McQueen takes to the western milieu as comfortably as Wayne, Cooper, or Eastwood ever did, and *Tom Horn* takes advantage of that partnership."

Unlike the actual Tom Horn, Steve showed through his acting ability and filmmaking abilities that he was able to evolve as to not be outlived by his own legend. "It's become a bit of a classic because [Tom Horn] has to do with individuality," Alonzo says. "More so, it has to do with McQueen. People realize what a great screen personality he was. He is garnering that kind of recognition purely on his ability, not on the dramatic way in which he died."

The actor and his craft.

Steve McQueen was one of hell's run away angels who rose up above the conditions he was born into and became one of cinemas most successful actors of all time. In his youth, he endured a neglectful mother and abusive stepfathers, life on the streets, gang violence, reform school, yearlong wanderings as a teen, and life in the Marines. Steve was constantly on the move searching for the place he belonged.

Eventually, Steve was able to find solace through the dedication and hard work of an actor. As a young man in the early 1950's Steve found a mentor and father figure in Sanford Meisner at The Neighborhood Playhouse. Under Sandy he learned the beginnings of acting technique that he would expand upon as he learned what worked for him throughout his life, boiling acting down to impulses and instincts.

Steve really did those things on camera he was portraying, not in any "Method" acting sense; he didn't need to go there. He listened when people spoke and often looked to physical actions as ways of bringing out authenticity. In doing so he brought authenticity to acting in a way that hadn't been seen before or since.

McQueen chose his films carefully and only played those roles he could identify with, which some people looked down upon. "Critics often wrote during his lifetime that Steve essentially played himself, but with the passage of time, he has proved them wrong," Steve's third wife Barbra said. "Nobody knew the endless hours and meticulous research he had put into preparing for his roles. In between takes, unlike a method actor, Steve could be himself. But as soon as the cameras rolled he became the person you saw on the screen."

There are common identifiers in the majority of Steve's roles as his grandson Steve R. McQueen noted, "He was the guy that was tough but without putting it in your face.

He was the guy that you don't wanna mess with, but you look up to him. And yeah as an actor those are the parts you wanna play!" There are common identifiers throughout the careers of every actor but this by no means indicates that they only play themselves. Look at Steve's roles in *The Thomas Crown Affair* and *Bullitt*, which both came out in 1968 where he plays on opposite sides of the law. As Thomas Crown, he is a Phi Beta Kappa playboy bank robber and as Detective Frank Bullitt he's a man birthed from the streets and immersed in the only thing he knows, violence.

Both were roles he could identify with, just like the up and coming card player in *The Cincinnati Kid*, the wrongfully accused and restless Frenchmen in *Papillon*, and the worldly cowboy who lived past his prime in *Tom Horn*. Throughout the course of his career, Steve McQueen continuously redefined himself on screen.

While Steve was redefining himself he was also redefining the role of the action hero altogether. During and after World War 2, movie goers flocked to see the good vs evil morality tales playing in theaters. But with the 60's came a greater complexity in cinema while Americans dealt with the civil rights movement, political assassinations, second wave feminism, and the Cold War. Films were becoming more morally ambiguous and so were their action heroes. Steve's performances like that of Jake Holman in *The Sand Pebbles* shows a man who would be content working on machinery but is thrust upon a clash of cultures where he chooses to shoot and kill his best friend because, ironically, that's the only way he can save him.

McQueen wasn't just portraying complex characters: his redefining of the action hero wasn't finished there. The 60's also saw the birth of "cool" of which Steve McQueen became the patron Saint. Steve didn't play the heroes of olden days where wealthy villains were defeated with wit, fancy foot work, and a saber, nor did he save damsels in distress for a peck on the cheek. He was the good bad guy who lived by a moral code set by himself and not society. In his films Steve gambled, cheated, drove fast, generally broke the rules whenever the act suited his cause, and audiences loved seeing him put safety third.

Steve did all these things on film and no matter how dire the situation got he remained cool. And even in his toughest moments taught audiences that there's a big difference between kneeling down and bending over. "A lot of actors are very animated and they create that expectation in the audience—and then they tire of it," Alec Baldwin noted. "The goal is economizing and McQueen understood that. The actor almost has to get out of the way. Don't do too much in movies, unless that's your signature. That 'take it or leave it' attitude he had is so compelling. How many men have made a career in the last thirty years of just looking into the camera and saying 'This is who I am and if you don't like it then too bad. And if you fire me tomorrow, I don't care."

To this day there is no actor that matches the McQueen persona. "Great looks, charisma, masculinity, vulnerability, menace. He had the fucking lot!" Gary Oldman exclaimed. And Ali McGraw took things up a notch when she said, "Every man I met wanted to be him, every woman wanted to sleep with him, every kid wanted to be mentored by him. He just had that extraordinary, charismatic, sort of sexual, but dangerous, but soft underneath, bright street smart, power."

McQueen was cool, period. He didn't care about being popular or following trends, he didn't care if he got dirt under his fingernails, and he certainly didn't need a group of "yes" men to follow him around. He was too busy to worry about what other people thought and he moved through life at such breakneck speed the only things that concerned him were the things right in front of him. Steve McQueen received his nickname "The King of Cool" only after his death when the rest of us finally caught up.

Sources

Introduction
-"I live for myself" www.imdb.com Steve McQueen Quotes

A Young McQueen
-"When a kid didn't have any love" www.imdb.com Steve McQueen Quotes
-"Westerns were my favorite" *Steve McQueen The Life And Legend Of A Hollywood Icon*, pp. 16
-"He apparently beat me for the sheer sadistic pleasure" *Steve McQueen The Life And Legend Of A Hollywood Icon*, pp. 22
-"To him, Los Angeles was at once fascinating" *My Husband, My Friend*, pp. 4
-"You should see some of life" *Steve McQueen Portrait of an American Rebel*, pp. 360
-"When one grows up in the streets" *Steve McQueen The Life And Legend Of A Hollywood Icon*, pp. 364
-"[Steve] was cut off emotionally" *Steve McQueen The Life And Legend Of A Hollywood Icon*, pp. 37
-"Nothing Without Labor." www.boysrepublic.org
-"Understanding is the magic word" and "Give life an honest shot" and "In that way, he laid" *Steve McQueen The Life And Legend Of A Hollywood Icon*, pp. 39
-"No one seemed to give a damn" *Steve McQueen The Life And Legend Of A Hollywood Icon*, pp. 39
-"Tough Shit" *Steve McQueen The Life And Legend Of A Hollywood Icon*, pp. 51
-"The Marines gave me discipline" *Steve McQueen The Life And Legend Of A Hollywood Icon*, pp. 54
-"For the first time in my life" and "It was a time when people lived" and "Things happened in the Village" *Steve McQueen Portrait of an American Rebel*, pp. 17
-I asked myself the bitter question" *Steve McQueen The Life And Legend Of A Hollywood Icon*, pp. 61

Steve's Early Acting Training.

-"I took stock of myself" and "I remember walking towards his office" *Steve McQueen A Biography by Marc Eliot*
-"He was an original" *Steve McQueen Portrait of an American Rebel*, pp. 19
-71 of 3,000 applicants *Steve McQueen The Life And Legend Of A Hollywood Icon*, pp. 62, *Steve McQueen A Biography by Marc Eliot*, pp. 25
-"Meisner preferred what he called 'untutored' students" *Steve McQueen A Tribute to The King Of Cool*, pp. 35
-"This is a school with no fancy frills" *Eli Wallach: The Good, the Bad, and Me*, pp. 53
-"Take it from a Director" *Sanford Meisner On Acting*, cover page
-"The foundation of acting" *Sanford Meisner On Acting*, pp. 16
-"Acting is the ability" Quoted by Martin Barter at The Sanford Meisner Center
-"Word Repetition Game" Sanford Meisner as quoted by Ranjiv Perera in an interview.
-"I decided I wanted an exercise" *Sanford Meisner On Acting*, pp. 36
-"Even then McQueen had the raw skill" *Steve McQueen The Actor And His Films*, pp. 100
-"If you'll stay with it" *Steve McQueen The Unauthorized Biography*
-"I don't think I was ever comfortable" *Sanford Meisner: Theater's Best-Kept Secret.*
-"I couldn't stand it" *Steve McQueen A Biography by Marc Eliot*, pp. 26
-"Until [Meisner] got after me" *Steve McQueen The Life And Legend Of A Hollywood Icon*, pp. 64
-"Candy-ass acting." *Steve McQueen A Tribute to The King Of Cool*, extra CD. 37 minute mark
-"Not yet. I'm still a student." *Steve McQueen The Life And Legend Of A Hollywood Icon*, pp. 67

-"I know that when I was studying" I AM STEVE MCQUEEN Documentary
-"He was badly educated, defensive, hostile." *Steve McQueen The Life And Legend Of A Hollywood Icon*, pp. 70
-"When it came to class" *Steve McQueen A Tribute to The King Of Cool*, pp. 34
-"All the things we were taught to do" *Steve McQueen The Life And Legend Of A Hollywood Icon*, pp. 71
-"At the beginning, back in '51" www.imdb.com Steve McQueen Quotes
-"father of method acting in America" www.strasberg.com
-"I would rather take my chances" *My Husband, My Friend*, pp. 41
-"Strasberg made an announcement" and "I used to be a Method School cowboy" *Steve McQueen The Life And Legend Of A Hollywood Icon*, pp. 97
-"Whatever he learned there" *Steve McQueen The Unauthorized Biography*
-"I'm an intuitive actor" I AM STEVE MCQUEEN Documentary
-"This man has made me weep" *On The Actors Art*, by Francois-Joseph Talma, 1883
-"I try very hard to try and get it out of myself" A Jack Linkletter interview in 1962

Steve's Fledgling Career.
-"I've got to make it. You're going to make it" *Steve McQueen The Life And Legend Of A Hollywood Icon*, pp. 72
-"Make no mistake" *Steve McQueen: The Cooler King*, pp. 13
-"I guess it was my lousy Yiddish." http://www.mcqueenonline.com/molly.htm
-"Effective" *My Husband, My Friend*, pp. 36
-"Put your left arm around my wrist" *My Husband, My Friend*, pp. 35

-"I saw innocence in his eyes" and "I ain't the marrying kind." *Steve McQueen Portrait of an American Rebel*, pp. 29

-"He liked this medium better" *My Husband, My Friend*, pp. 41

-"There are too many blond-haired" *Steve McQueen The Life And Legend Of A Hollywood Icon*, pp. 102 and *My Husband, My Friend*, pp. 60

-"This was the first time" *My Husband, My Friend*, pp. 62

-"Character is habitual action" *True and False by David Mamet*

-"I remember watching McQueen" *Steve McQueen The Life And Legend Of A Hollywood Icon*, pp. 103

-"The acting was uniformly expert" *Steve McQueen A Biography by Marc Eliot*, pp. 41

-"I saw one minute" *Steve McQueen The Life And Legend Of A Hollywood Icon*, pp. 102

Wanted: Dead or Alive season 1

-"I needed a little guy" and "I chose him because" *Wanted Dead or Alive* DVD special features.

-Hilly's thoughts on Steve transitioning to television. *Steve McQueen Portrait of an American Rebel*, pp. 39

-Info on Steve booking the role of Josh Randall *My Husband, My Friend*, pp. 73

-"[Randall] seemed to be a loner" *Steve McQueen The Life And Legend Of A Hollywood Icon*, pp. 120

-"They thought all cowboys" *Steve McQueen Portrait of an American Rebel*, pp. 45

-"The fans don't care" *Steve McQueen Portrait of an American Rebel*, pp. 45 and *Steve McQueen The Life And Legend Of A Hollywood Icon*, pp. 124

-"I was mesmerized" *The Last Mile*, pp. 17

-*Wanted Dead or Alive* quickly rose to one of the top ten, *My Husband, My Friend*, pp. 81

-"These early reviews only made Steve" *My Husband, My Friend*, pp.78-79

-"Every bit of energy he expended"
-"The scripts being given him" *My Husband, My Friend,* pp. 76
-"Look, I'm not going to fight" *Steve McQueen Portrait of an American Rebel,* pp. 46
-"A fistfight was about to ensue" *My Husband, My Friend,* pp. 76
-"When a horse learns" *Steve McQueen A Biography by Marc Eliot,* pp.
-"They gave me this real old horse" *Steve McQueen The Life And Legend Of A Hollywood Icon,* pp. 121 and *Steve McQueen Portrait of an American Rebel,* pp. 45
-"It was wild" *Steve McQueen Portrait of an American Rebel,* pp. 46
-"For three long years" *Steve McQueen The Life And Legend Of A Hollywood Icon,* pp. 122
-"You don't have any idea" *Steve McQueen Portrait of an American Rebel,* pp. 57 and *Steve McQueen The Life And Legend Of A Hollywood Icon,* pp. 147
-"They'd roll the cameras" *Steve McQueen The Life And Legend Of A Hollywood Icon,* pp. 123
-"We are a bakery" *Steve McQueen The Life And Legend Of A Hollywood Icon,* pp. 148
-"Any actor who works on a TV show" *Steve McQueen Portrait of an American Rebel,* pp. 45
-"Steve learned what very few actors know" *Steve McQueen Portrait of an American Rebel,* pp. 412
-Neile about Steve's on camera experimenting.

Never So Few
-"It had always been our plan" *Steve McQueen Portrait of an American Rebel,* pp. 38
-"Give the kid all the close-ups." *Steve McQueen A Biography by Marc Eliot,* pp. 68
-"Steve McQueen looks good" *The New York Herald Tribune*

Wanted: Dead or Alive seasons 2 & 3

-"I worked hard" www.imdb.com Steve McQueen Quotes
-"When you're hot" *Steve McQueen A Biography by Marc Eliot*, pp. 52
-"He obviously got a bad reputation" *Steve McQueen Portrait of an American Rebel*, pp. 47
-"Randall was the blueprint" *Steve McQueen A Tribute to The King Of Cool*, pp 66
-"His brand of masculinity" *Steve McQueen A Tribute to The King Of Cool*, pp 203
-"Steve isn't argumentative" *Steve McQueen Portrait of an American Rebel*, pp. 47
-"One mistake I made" *Steve McQueen The Life And Legend Of A Hollywood Icon*, pp. 140
-"Steve was a perfectionist" *Steve McQueen Portrait of an American Rebel*, pp. 44
-"The market was going" *Steve McQueen Portrait of an American Rebel*, pp. 64
-"While Steve was relieved" *My Husband, My Friend*, pp. 97
-"Hell, no! I was delighted" *Steve McQueen Portrait of an American Rebel*, pp. 65

The Magnificent Seven

-"Movie acting is reacting" *Steve McQueen The Actor And His Films*, pp 103 and *Eli Wallach: The Good, the Bad, and Me*, pp 203
-"When [McQueen] walked into my office"*Escape Artist: The Life and Films of John Sturges*, pp 167
-"I promise" *Steve McQueen The Actor And His Films*, pp 99 and *Steve McQueen Portrait of an American Rebel*, pp. 58
-"John Sturges was one of the few men" *Steve McQueen Portrait of an American Rebel*, pp. 58
-"Have an accident" *Steve McQueen The Life And Legend Of A Hollywood Icon*, pp. 155
-"It was only a matter of seconds" *My Husband, My Friend*

-"[Sturges] enjoyed so much" *The Magnificent Seven* movie commentary.

-"I just picked out whatever" *Escape Artist: The Life and Films of John Sturges*, pp 198

-"Those rooms were always" *Steve McQueen: The Cooler King*, pp 121

-"You were free within that form" *The Magnificent Seven* movie commentary.

-"As far as directing the actors" *Escape Artist: The Life and Films of John Sturges*, pp 203

-"What I liked as an actor" *The Magnificent Seven* movie commentary.

-"The basic thing was that" *The Magnificent Seven* behind the scenes documentary.

-"Each one of them did" *Steve McQueen: The Cooler King*, pp. 122

-"catching flies" *Escape Artist: The Life and Films of John Sturges*, pp 206

-"When you work in a scene with Yul" *Steve McQueen Portrait of an American Rebel*, pp. 60 and *Steve McQueen A Biography by Marc Eliot*, pp. 81

-"Steve's main aim was to promote" *Steve McQueen Portrait of an American Rebel*, pp. 60

-"He wanted me to use a rifle" *Steve McQueen Portrait of an American Rebel*, pp. 60

-"Steve and Yul Brynner weren't that tall" *Steve McQueen The Life And Legend Of A Hollywood Icon*, pp. 158 and *Steve McQueen Portrait of an American Rebel*, pp. 60

-"He was paranoid about Yul" and "One time he said to me" *Steve McQueen The Life And Legend Of A Hollywood Icon*, pp. 157 and *Steve McQueen A Tribute to The King Of Cool*, pp. 82

-"Yul was then a very big star" *Steve McQueen: The Cooler King*, pp. 125

-"All they wanted to do were cowboy movies." *The Magnificent Seven* behind the scenes documentary.

-"I think you'd be able to tell" *Steve McQueen: The Cooler*

King, pp. 127
-"Steve wasn't what you would call" *Steve McQueen A Biography by Marc Eliot*, pp. 62 and *Steve McQueen The Life And Legend Of A Hollywood Icon*, pp. 159
-"They're dissimilar characters" *Steve McQueen The Life And Legend Of A Hollywood Icon*, pp. 159
-"It was a wonderful competitive" *Steve McQueen A Tribute to The King Of Cool*, pp. 83
-"When Steve pushed his hat" *Escape Artist: The Life and Films of John Sturges*, pp 207
-"I had more fun on that picture" *The Magnificent Seven* behind the scenes documentary.
-"That movie made Steve a star" and "We were so busy hating you" *Steve McQueen Portrait of an American Rebel*, pp. 63

Hell Is For Heroes & The War Lover
-"I have to stay in character." and "I always try to immerse" *Steve McQueen The Life And Legend Of A Hollywood Icon*, pp. 179 and *Steve McQueen Portrait of an American Rebel*, pp. 77
-"It's the most perceptive" *Steve McQueen A Biography by Marc Eliot*, pp. 101 and *Steve McQueen The Life And Legend Of A Hollywood Icon*, pp. 170
-"Man, I like you guys" *Steve McQueen The Actor And His Films*, pp 124 and *Steve McQueen The Life And Legend Of A Hollywood Icon*, pp. 169
-"McQueen was definitive" *Steve McQueen A Tribute to The King Of Cool*, pp. 94
Malfunctioning M3 gun. *Steve McQueen A Biography by Marc Eliot*, pp. 98
-"Anyone who steps over" *Steve McQueen The Life And Legend Of A Hollywood Icon*, pp. 170
-"A kind of schizophrenic" *Steve McQueen The Life And Legend Of A Hollywood Icon*, pp. 181

The Great Escape

-"If they were making a movie" I AM STEVE MCQUEEN Documentary

-"It was about why our side won" *Escape Artist: The Life and Films of John Sturges*, pp. 224

-"Where's my thing?" *Steve McQueen The Life And Legend Of A Hollywood Icon*, pp. 192

-"He had to find his niche." *Steve McQueen: The Cooler King*, pp. 173

-"The part of Virgil Hilts" *My Husband, My Friend*, pp. 106

-"He was groping around" *Escape Artist: The Life and Films of John Sturges*, pp 232

-"I'm getting tired of arguing with you" *Steve McQueen The Life And Legend Of A Hollywood Icon*, pp. 195-197

-"I saw Steve a few times" *Steve McQueen: The Cooler King*, pp. 173

-"Steve wanted to be the hero" *Steve McQueen A Biography by Marc Eliot*, pp. 120 and *Steve McQueen A Tribute to The King Of Cool*, pp. 111

-"I'm going to do this perfectly or die trying." Quoted by Martin Barter at The Sanford Meisner Center

-"I spent a whole day in that cell" *Steve McQueen: The Cooler King*, pp. 176

-"That was all written in" *Steve McQueen: The Cooler King*, pp. 175

-"Once those additions" *Steve McQueen: The Cooler King*, pp. 178

-Steve accepting the role to showcase his motorcycle skills. www.imdb.com and *The Great Escape: The Flight to Freedom* Documentary

-"When you find somebody" *Steve McQueen A Biography by Marc Eliot*, pp. 121 and *Steve McQueen Portrait of an American Rebel*, pp. 91

-Having gym equipment at all the filming locations over two weeks. *My Husband, My Friend*, pp. 109

-"The British would always" *Steve McQueen The Life And Legend Of A Hollywood Icon*, pp. 199

-"There was a raw vulnerability" *The Great Escape* Bluray

commentary
-"He was forever fighting" *Steve McQueen A Tribute to The King Of Cool*, pp. 115
-"He would get more" *The Great Escape* Bluray commentary
-"Steve liked to watch the scene" *Steve McQueen Portrait of an American Rebel*, pp. 84
-"One of the best screen actors of all time." *Steve McQueen A Tribute to The King Of Cool*, pp. 115
-"It was a great chance" *Steve McQueen: The Cooler King*, pp. 168
-"It didn't cause other people happiness" *Steve McQueen Portrait of an American Rebel*, pp. 84
-"Steve was very professional" *Steve McQueen The Life And Legend Of A Hollywood Icon*, pp. 85
-"Steve's performance was perfect in the film" *Steve McQueen A Biography by Marc Eliot*, pp. 119

Love With The Proper Stranger
-"They call me a chauvinist pig" www.imdb.com Steve McQueen Quotes
-"Character comes from how you feel about something." Sanford Meisner On Acting, pp. 93
-"It showed all the aspects" *Steve McQueen The Life And Legend Of A Hollywood Icon*, pp. 204
-"Steve McQueen contributes a quieter" *Films and Filming*

Overcoming impediments
-"I believe in me" www.imdb.com Steve McQueen Quotes
-The 2014 poll taken. I conducted this poll with all of my actor friends and classmates.
-Steve having dyslexia. *Steve McQueen The Actor And His Films*, pp. 428
-"I have to be careful because I'm a limited actor" www.imdb.com Steve McQueen Quotes
-Contrasting himself with Laurence Olivier *Steve McQueen The Life And Legend Of A Hollywood Icon*, pp.

331
-"Technique, at this point" *My Husband, My Friend*
-"Later on, as a movie star" *My Husband, My Friend*
-"His power came from his facial expressions" *Steve McQueen A Tribute to The King Of Cool*, pp. 239

The Cincinnati Kid
-"Steve comes out of the tradition" *Steve McQueen Portrait of an American Rebel*, pp. 117
-Neile saying he never missed a Bogart or Cagney movie. *My Husband, My Friend*, pp. 37
-"I know things are still up" *Steve McQueen: The Cooler King*, pp. 231
-"When I took on the task of directing" *Steve McQueen The Actor And His Films*, pp. 228
-"For me, the movie was about winning" *Norman Jewison: This Terrible Business Has Been Good to Me*, pg. 97
-"Just give him some money" *Steve McQueen: The Cooler King*, pp. 232
-"Steve McQueen realized he had a big challenge" and "I'd been away from the camera" *Steve McQueen: The Cooler King*, pp. 235
-"After so much time away from acting" *My Husband, My Friend*, pp. 119
-"Remember, McQueen embraced Sam" *Steve McQueen Portrait of an American Rebel*, pp. 116
-"In the early scenes we shot" and "I'm the guy who's always around taking" and "Why do you want to watch them" and "We ran the scenes for him" *Norman Jewison: This Terrible Business Has Been Good to Me*, pg. 103
-"McQueen sprung at me like a tiger" *Steve McQueen: Man on the Edge* Documentary
-"Our director, Henry Hathaway" *Karl Malden: When Do I Start*, pg. 299
-"[Edward G.] certainly wasn't a man to be rattled" *Norman Jewison: This Terrible Business Has Been Good to Me*, pg. 106

-"[Steve] was a little nervous" *Steve McQueen: The Cooler King*, pp. 235
-"Look at your entrance" *Norman Jewison: This Terrible Business Has Been Good to Me*, pg. 105
-"All around that table sat a really solid" *Karl Malden: When Do I Start*, pg. 298
-"Everyone around that poker table could"
-"You better watch out" and "Watch the kid." and "Young star against the old star" *The Cincinnati Kid* directors commentary
-"Shit-kicking actor" *Steve McQueen: The Essence of Cool* Documentary
-"For Steve to predict that was very interesting" and "Norman and I were looking at each other" *Steve McQueen: The Cooler King*, pp. 237
-"I could hardly speak the words" *Steve McQueen: The Cooler King*, pp. 236
-"I have nightmares about being poor" *Steve McQueen Portrait of an American Rebel*, pp. 111
-*The New and Improved Leading Man by Mark Harris, http://www.gq.com*
-"Success as an actor" *Steve McQueen Portrait of an American Rebel*, pp. 263
-"What I chose to see in Steve" *Moving Pictures by Ali MacGraw*, pp. 92

The Sandpebbles

-"For me, to do some of these scenes" *Steve McQueen: Man on the Edge* Documentary
-Neile said she never saw Steve work as hard as he did on *The Sand Pebbles. Steve McQueen Portrait of an American Rebel*, pp. 141
-Steve was originally the 7th choice to play Jake Holman. *Steve McQueen: The Cooler King*, pp. 261-265
-"He had a great understanding" *Steve McQueen: The Cooler King*, pp. 268
-"His whole being" *The Sandpebbles* DVD special

features.

-"You know young actors could sit" and "He was born to play this role" *The Sandpebbles* DVD Commentary.

-"I'd often wondered if a tank" *Steve McQueen The Life And Legend Of A Hollywood Icon*, pp. 50

-Had his gym equipment shipped to the filming location. *Steve McQueen Portrait of an American Rebel*, pp. 132

-"I think the sequence where Holman" *Steve McQueen: The Cooler King*, pp. 269

-None of Steve's takes were used. *Steve McQueen The Life And Legend Of A Hollywood Icon*, pp. 242

-The McQueen and Crenna meeting. *Steve McQueen A Biography by Marc Eliot*, pp. 171 and *Steve McQueen The Life And Legend Of A Hollywood Icon*, pp. 242

-Marshall Terrill saying that not a single one of the Steve's takes were used. *Steve McQueen The Life And Legend Of A Hollywood Icon*, pp. 242

-"Are you going to do that" and "In a few days' time" *Steve McQueen: The Cooler King*, pp. 269

-The Wise and McQueen confrontation and "Here I was directing the star of the film." *Steve McQueen: Man on the Edge* Documentary and *The Sandpebbles* DVD Commentary.

-"Nobody knows this but" *Steve McQueen: The Cooler King*, pp. 237

-"Most actors play it up" *Steve McQueen The Life And Legend Of A Hollywood Icon*, pp. 85

-"The Reality of Doing" As taught by Martin Barter at The Sanford Meisner Center.

-"Play Acting" *Steve McQueen The Life And Legend Of A Hollywood Icon*, pp. 395 and *Steve McQueen A Tribute to The King Of Cool*, pp. 271

-"Because he used his own personality" *The Sandpebbles* DVD special features.

-"I've never worked with a star"

-"the most restrained" *Steve McQueen A Biography by Marc Eliot*, pp. 183 and *Steve McQueen The Actor And*

His Films, pp. 271
-"[He] brought a tremendous" and "McQueen has a cerebral vitality" *Steve McQueen: The Cooler King*, pp. 277
-"McQueen is a unique actor" *The Hollywood Reporter*
-"If he'd won, he'd have been impossible" *My Husband, My Friend*
-"Ah fuck 'em all, next time we get 'em." *Steve McQueen: The Cooler King*, pp. 274

The Thomas Crown Affair
-"I believe in lots of preparation" *Steve McQueen Portrait of an American Rebel*, pp. 151
-"A love story between two shits." and "Style over content" *The Thomas Crown Affair* DVD Commentary
-"They went after Connery" *Steve McQueen: The Cooler King*, pp. 279-297
-"I thought of changing" *Steve McQueen Portrait of an American Rebel*, pp. 148
-"Gee honey that's too bad," "What are you talking about," and "Well you know Norman" *Steve McQueen: Man on the Edge* Documentary
-"Over my dead body" and "I was advised not to do it" *Steve McQueen: The Cooler King*, pp. 279-297
-"Steve McQueen grew up in boys town" *The Thomas Crown Affair* DVD Commentary
-"When I heard McQueen was cast" *Steve McQueen: The Cooler King*, pp. 279-297
-"By the end of that week" and "I don't know how, but the son of a bitch knows me."*Steve McQueen: The Cooler King*, pp. 279-297
-Jewison's direction to try a "clipped" accent. *The Thomas Crown Affair* DVD Commentary
-"On the first day of rehearsing" *My Husband, My Friend*
-Steve calling Faye Dunaway "Dun-fade-away" *The Thomas Crown Affair* DVD Commentary
-"We had both grown up on the wrong side" and "Steve

had so much charisma" *Steve McQueen: The Cooler King*, pp. 279-297

-Information on Jewison filming the chess scene. *The Thomas Crown Affair* DVD Commentary

-"Jewison had McQueen doing what" *Steve McQueen The Life And Legend Of A Hollywood Icon*, pp. 257

-"If you put Steve on an empty stage" *Steve McQueen A Tribute to The King Of Cool*, pp. 131

-"Steve dislikes open emotions" *Steve McQueen The Unauthorized Biography*

'Bullitt'

-"I don't know a young actor" *Steve McQueen: The Essence of Cool* Documentary

-"We had been at Warner's" *Steve McQueen: The Cooler King*, pp. 298-329

-"No way I'm playin' a cop" *Steve McQueen The Life And Legend Of A Hollywood Icon*, pp. 263

-"[Pike's] book was about a 67-year-old" *Steve McQueen: The Cooler King*, pp. 298-329

-Robert Vaughn turning down the role of Walter Chalmers. *Steve McQueen The Life And Legend Of A Hollywood Icon*, pp. 264

-"Do you know what a hook is" *Steve McQueen The Life And Legend Of A Hollywood Icon*, pp. 264

-Trustman left the project after a few too many changes were made. *Steve McQueen: The Cooler King*, pp. 298-329

-"Good he'll be home" *Steve McQueen The Life And Legend Of A Hollywood Icon*, pp. 264

-"Peter had tremendous enthusiasm" *Steve McQueen: The Cooler King*, pp. 298-329

-"Why does Steve want to do a movie about a cop" *Steve McQueen The Life And Legend Of A Hollywood Icon*, pp. 265

-"I think that more so than any other time" *Steve McQueen The Life And Legend Of A Hollywood Icon*, pp. 265

-"We're trying to show what a cop could be like" *Steve McQueen Portrait of an American Rebel*, pp. 161

-"There had been too many police pictures made" Bullitt DVD Commentary

-"If he got a script and they told him" *Steve McQueen Portrait of an American Rebel*, pp. 165

-"It was [McQueen's] first picture as a producer" Bullitt DVD Commentary

-"Sure we could shoot in the studio" *Steve McQueen The Actor And His Films*, pp. 318

-Information on shooting in San Francisco. *Bullitt Points: Memories of Steve McQueen and Bullitt*

-"The feelings, the sensitivities" *Bullitt: Steve McQueen's Commitment to Reality: The Making of 'Bullitt'*

-"I think the film should be of a more impressionistic" *Steve McQueen Portrait of an American Rebel*, pp. 164

-"lodgings for alcoholics" *Bullitt Points: Memories of Steve McQueen and Bullitt*

-"That hotel really was a hotel" *Steve McQueen: The Cooler King*, pp. 298-329

-Hiding things in the hotel room for Steve to find. *Bullitt Points: Memories of Steve McQueen and Bullitt*

-"He was a tough guy" *Steve McQueen A Tribute to The King Of Cool*, pp. 38

-"I'm a reactor, don't give me too" and "Dealt very well with dialogue" Bullitt DVD Commentary

-"You could always rely on McQueen" Bullitt DVD Commentary

-"I don't want to talk, give the speeches" *Steve McQueen: The Cooler King*, pp. 298-329

-"You only say what's important" www.imdb.com Steve McQueen Quotes

-"I have a good feeling" *Steve McQueen Portrait of an American Rebel*, pp. 162

-"Over the years Steve had developed" *My Husband, My Friend*, pp. 161

-"I wanted to see the inside" *Steve McQueen The Actor*

And His Films, pp. 308 and *Bullitt Points: Memories of Steve McQueen and Bullitt*

-"The police took me in there" Bullitt DVD Commentary

-"The officers went into a strange state" *Steve McQueen Portrait of an American Rebel*, pp. 161

-"He felt it gave the actors more control" and "Got up and made a really lovely speech." Bullitt DVD Commentary

-"You know, this shows people" Bullitt DVD Commentary

-"Movie stars are essentially canvases" *Steve McQueen A Tribute to The King Of Cool*, pp. 203

-"That again was an idea of Steve's" and "I think I should take one of everything" Bullitt DVD Commentary

-"That's a quiet no dialogue moment" Bullitt DVD Commentary

-"McQueen's movement is extraordinary" Bullitt DVD Commentary

-Peter packed the prop trunks so that Steve and Don wouldn't know exactly what's in them. And them practicing with real detectives beforehand. Bullitt DVD Commentary

-Peter saying that they loved playing the scene of them opening the trunks looking for cues. Bullitt DVD Commentary

-"We chose Jacqueline Bisset for the film" *Bullitt: Steve McQueen's Commitment to Reality: The Making of 'Bullitt'*

-"We were using her as a comment" Bullitt DVD Commentary

-Filming the Coffee Cantata scene. *Bullitt: Steve McQueen's Commitment to Reality: The Making of 'Bullitt'*

-"I suppose I was the aesthetic part of his life." *Steve McQueen: The Cooler King*, pp. 298-329

-"Steve and I were great admirers of drivers" Bullitt DVD Commentary

-"During interviews, Steve talked a lot" *My Husband, My Friend*, pp. 187

-"I've got a feeling I'm leaving stardom behind" http://www.stevemcqueensite.com/stevemcqueenquotes.htm

The Getaway

-"Insecurity is pretty good motivation." *I AM STEVE MCQUEEN* Documentary

-The First Artist deal Steve made. *Steve McQueen The Life And Legend Of A Hollywood Icon*, pp. 328

-"For years, I'd been bugging Steve" *Steve McQueen Portrait of an American Rebel*, pp. 220

-"I knew Steve had always wanted" and "Lock it up." *Steve McQueen The Life And Legend Of A Hollywood Icon*, pp. 348

-"I went to Peckinpah on the idea" *Steve McQueen The Life And Legend Of A Hollywood Icon*, pp. 349

-"Of course to do one picture" 1972 Reel 1 - "Virtual" Audio Commentary on *The Getaway blu ray*

-"[McQueen] wanted to be as real" *I AM STEVE MCQUEEN* Documentary

-"I sorta lived with them" and "We all decided the look" 1972 Reel 1 - "Virtual" Audio Commentary on *The Getaway blu ray*

-"I first saw Bogart on the screen" *Steve McQueen Portrait of an American Rebel*, pp. 221

-"Steve was totally careful about realism" *Steve McQueen Portrait of an American Rebel*, pp. 238-239

-"It's going to be difficult for me" *Steve McQueen The Life And Legend Of A Hollywood Icon*, pp. 348

-"I watched him act closely on the set" *Steve McQueen: The Cooler King*, pp. 567

-"Watching him perform was a trip" *Steve McQueen The Life And Legend Of A Hollywood Icon*, pp. 338

-"If you really want to learn about acting" *I AM STEVE MCQUEEN* Documentary

-"When reading the script" *Steve McQueen Portrait of an American Rebel*, pp. 238-239

-"And that was what you wrote seven pages of dialogue to explain?" And, "Well, you know better than to listen to me, Sam." *Steve McQueen Portrait of an American Rebel*, pp. 238

-"He's a great great great film actor" 1972 Reel 1 - "Virtual" Audio Commentary on *The Getaway blu ray*
-"Lawyers sharpen up with law books" *Steve McQueen Portrait of an American Rebel*, pp. 132 and *Steve McQueen A Biography by Marc Eliot*, pp. 189
-"I don't think anybody ever handled guns" *Steve McQueen The Life And Legend Of A Hollywood Icon*, pp. 238
-"Steve's military training" *The Last Mile*, pp. 85
-Bruce calling himself the "Oriental Steve McQueen." *Steve McQueen Portrait of an American Rebel*, pp. 181
-"If you ever want to take karate lessons" *Steve McQueen The Life And Legend Of A Hollywood Icon*, pp. 364
-"McQueen, that son of a gun" 9 December 1971 *The Pierre Berton Show* Interview of Bruce Lee
-"Steve was probably the most aggressive guy" *I AM STEVE MCQUEEN* Documentary
-"Steve didn't hold anything back" *Steve McQueen Portrait of an American Rebel*, pp. 240
-"Steve and Sam had a strange relationship" *Steve McQueen: The Cooler King*, pp. 408
-"McQueen's playing it safe" *Steve McQueen Portrait of an American Rebel*, pp. 244 and *Steve McQueen The Life And Legend Of A Hollywood Icon*, pp. 367
-"*The Getaway* was my first attempt" *Peckinpah: A Portrait in Montage*, pp. 157
-"*The Getaway* meant more to me in a financial and professional way" *Steve McQueen Portrait of an American Rebel*, pp. 246
-"We fought all the time." *Steve McQueen: The Cooler King*, pp. 439

Papillon
-"I'm tired of being the chief" *Steve McQueen Portrait of an American Rebel*, pp. 212
-"I do it by instinct" *Steve McQueen Portrait of an American Rebel*, pp. 143

-"My argument had been if all the actors" *My Husband, My Friend,* pp. 287

-"Let the producer do his thing" *My Husband, My Friend,* pp. 287

-"When we began shooting" *Steve McQueen The Life And Legend Of A Hollywood Icon,* pp. 376

-"He was the best director" *Steve McQueen: The Cooler King,* pp. 463

-"He and Steve became quite close" *Steve McQueen: The Cooler King,* pp. 464

-"[McQueen] always played with such mystery" *I AM STEVE MCQUEEN* Documentary

-"I kept being driven by this restless feeling" *Steve McQueen Portrait of an American Rebel,* pp. 263 and *Steve McQueen The Life And Legend Of A Hollywood Icon,* pp. 375 and *Steve McQueen The Actor And His Films,* pp. 428

-"He was one of those natural actors" *Steve McQueen: The Cooler King,* pp. 602

-"Steve McQueen was a very intense man" Emanuel L. Wolf *Steve McQueen: The Cooler King,* pp. 604

-"If a guy like [Dustin Hoffman] can become a star" www.imdb.com Steve McQueen Quotes

-Dustin was considered the least likely to succeed by his acting class. *Papillon* Bluray booklet

-Dustin was eating only one-half to one full coconut a day. *Steve McQueen A Biography by Marc Eliot,* pp. 269 and *Ali MacGraw: Moving Pictures,* pp. 102 and *Steve McQueen The Actor And His Films,* pp. 422 and *Steve McQueen The Life And Legend Of A Hollywood Icon,* pp. 378

-"I would always shoot on McQueen first" *Steve McQueen The Actor And His Films,* pp. 422 and *Steve McQueen Portrait of an American Rebel,* pp. 262

-"As a cameraman, you can't get" *Steve McQueen: The Cooler King,* pp. 466

-"Steve worked hard on *Papillon*" *Steve McQueen Portrait*

of an American Rebel, pp. 262

-"There was this young guy" *Steve McQueen: The Cooler King*, pp. 465

-"Ever since Steve had seen Eli" *My Husband, My Friend*, pp. 287

-"I've cut everything down" *Steve McQueen The Life And Legend Of A Hollywood Icon*, pp. 331

-"[McQueen] walks onto the screen and he kidnaps you." *I AM STEVE MCQUEEN* Documentary

-"Dustin Hoffman used to come into the projection room" and "By the time Steve did *Papillon*" *Steve McQueen: The Cooler King*, pp. 467

-"Less Dusty. Do less" *Steve McQueen Portrait of an American Rebel*, pp. 262 and *Steve McQueen The Actor And His Films*, pp. 423

-"Both of us were suspicious" *Steve McQueen The Life And Legend Of A Hollywood Icon*, pp. 376

-"If you're going to do a part" *Steve McQueen The Actor And His Films*, pp. 272

-Steve practiced getting and out of his Porsche for six hours straight. And "He wanted it to look normal to him" *Steve McQueen Portrait of an American Rebel*, pp. 194

-"When I think of McQueen as an actor" *Steve McQueen The Actor And His Films*, pp. 429 and *Steve McQueen A Tribute to The King Of Cool*, pp. 256

-"In our scene together" *Steve McQueen The Life And Legend Of A Hollywood Icon*, pp. 377 and *Steve McQueen A Tribute to The King Of Cool*, pp. 256

-"I felt Charrière should have some kind of physical handicap" *Steve McQueen Portrait of an American Rebel*, pp. 266

-"All of that work for him was very tough" *Steve McQueen Portrait of an American Rebel*, pp. 264

-"I think he probably worked harder as an actor" *Steve McQueen: The Cooler King*, pp. 456

-"He was very proud of his work in *Papillon*" *Steve McQueen: The Cooler King*, pp. 456

-*Papillon* would become the fourth highest earning film of 1973 and the most successful film ever made by Allied Artists. *Steve McQueen The Actor And His Films*, pp. 424

-"Whatever anyone might say about Steve" *Steve McQueen: The Cooler King*, pp. 475

-"Acting styles go through changes" *Steve McQueen Portrait of an American Rebel*, pp. 433

Tom Horn

-"You only go around once in life" *I AM STEVE MCQUEEN* Documentary

-Roles Steve turned down. *Steve McQueen Portrait of an American Rebel*, pp. 287

-"Steve McQueen was 47 years old" *The Last Mile*, pp. 11

-"I wanted to do *An Enemy of the People*" *Steve McQueen The Life And Legend Of A Hollywood Icon*, pp. 417

-"For the first time in my life" *Steve McQueen Portrait of an American Rebel*, pp. 296

-"At this stage in my life" *Steve McQueen A Biography by Marc Eliot*, pp. 296

-"I've always wanted to do Horn's story" *Steve McQueen The Life And Legend Of A Hollywood Icon*, pp. 420 and *Steve McQueen Portrait of an American Rebel*, pp. 318

-"Time had passed him by" *Steve McQueen Portrait of an American Rebel*, pp. 320

-"Steve wanted to take the books home" *Steve McQueen The Life And Legend Of A Hollywood Icon*, pp. 421

-"He wanted to talk constantly" *Steve McQueen: The Cooler King*, pp. 523

-"Despite all his previous success" *Steve McQueen The Actor And His Films*, pp. 463

-"The whole introduction of Horn" and "I don't believe in any of this business" *Steve McQueen The Actor And His Films*, pp. 466

-"Steve was okay about it" *Steve McQueen: The Cooler King*, pp. 531

-"When Steve gave me the script" *Steve McQueen: The*

Cooler King, pp. 520

-"I have a feeling that I'm very well" *Steve McQueen Portrait of an American Rebel*, pp. 320

-"I believe the secret to Steve's success" *The Last Mile*, pp. 113

-"I try not to take myself too seriously" *Steve McQueen The Life And Legend Of A Hollywood Icon*, pp. 395 and *Steve McQueen A Tribute to The King Of Cool*, pp. 271 and

-"He took all the stuntmen cowboys" *Steve McQueen: The Cooler King*, pp. 529

-"I just wanna see if I can pick up" *The Last Mile*

-"I'm completely against this " *Steve McQueen Portrait of an American Rebel*, pp. 322

-"I don't think this is going to work" *Steve McQueen Portrait of an American Rebel*, pp. 330

-"The film company didn't seem to be able to settle" *Steve McQueen A Tribute to The King Of Cool*, pp. 320

-Reports from those on set said that for the most part Wiard stood around like a production assistant. *Steve McQueen A Tribute to The King Of Cool*, pp. 319

-"Steve had both scripts in his hands" *Steve McQueen Portrait of an American Rebel*, pp. 322

-"On my first take as the Judge" *Steve McQueen: The Cooler King*, pp. 528

-"He would listen to people" *Steve McQueen: The Cooler King*, pp. 527

-"[McQueen's] a better actor than people think" *Steve McQueen Portrait of an American Rebel*, pp. 350

-"On *The Magnificent Seven*, he was a young" *Steve McQueen Portrait of an American Rebel*, pp. 320

-"Now that Steve was closing in on 50" *The Last Mile*, pp. 193

-"It's a film about a hero" *Steve McQueen A Tribute to The King Of Cool*, pp. 346

-"Many evenings we'd go over his lines" *The Last Mile*, pp. 129

-"It takes twenty years to become a master." As quoted by Martin Barter at The Sanford Meisner Center
-"His power came from his facial expressions" *Steve McQueen A Tribute to The King Of Cool*, pp. 239
-"*Tom Horn*, I thought was Steve's best film" *Steve McQueen The Actor And His Films*, pp. 467 and *Steve McQueen Portrait of an American Rebel*, pp. 337
-"McQueen's positive attitude and passion" *Steve McQueen A Tribute to The King Of Cool*, pp. 319
-"Steve changed my opinion of actors" *Steve McQueen A Tribute to The King Of Cool*, pp. 320
-"When I believe in something" www.imdb.com
-"He had a great visionary mind" *Steve McQueen: The Cooler King*, pp. 523
-"Warners Didn't want it" *Steve McQueen Portrait of an American Rebel*, pp. 335
-"Steve McQueen, after a six-year absence" *The Hollywood Reporter,* March 28th 1980
-"It's become a bit of a classic" *Steve McQueen Portrait of an American Rebel*, pp. 336

The actor and his craft.

-"Critics often wrote during his lifetime" *The Last Mile*, pp. 119
-"He was the guy that was tough" *I AM STEVE MCQUEEN* Documentary
-"A lot of actors are very animated" *Steve McQueen A Tribute to The King Of Cool*, pp. 259
-"Great looks, charisma" and "Every man I met wanted to be him" *I AM STEVE MCQUEEN* Documentary
-"Me a legend?" *Steve McQueen A Biography by Marc Eliot*, pp. 263

Made in the USA
Coppell, TX
28 December 2021

70305932R00111